A sketch of the Parish of Prestbury.

George Yarnold Osborne

A sketch of the Parish of Prestbury.
Osborne, George Yarnold
British Library, Historical Print Editions
British Library
1840
8°.
10368.f.8.

E. Hawkins Esq

British Museum

with Geo. & Osborne

Comp.ts

May 29. 1840

ERRATUM.

Page 16, line 33, for Viaduct, read Aqueduct.

SKETCH

OF THE

PARISH OF PRESTBURY.

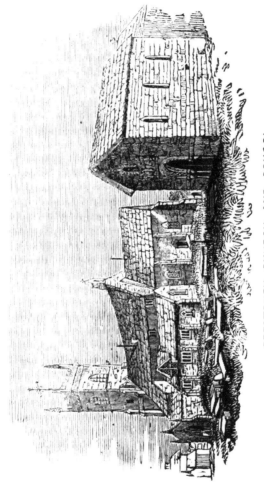

PRESTBURY CHURCH AND SCHOOL.

A

SKETCH

OF THE

PARISH OF PRESTBURY.

BY GEORGE YARNOLD OSBORNE.

This while my notion's ta'en a sklent
To try my luck in gude black prent,
    Something cries ' Hoolie!
I red you, honest mon, tak tent,
    Ye'll shaw your folly !'—BURNS.

MACCLESFIELD:

TO

JOHN UPTON GASKELL, ESQ.

OF INGERSLEY HALL,

A TRUE FRIEND,

A KIND MASTER, AN HONEST MAN;

THIS TRIFLE

IS AFFECTIONATELY INSCRIBED BY

THE AUTHOR.

PREFACE.

———◆———

Gentle Reader,

    I know thee not, and yet, methinks, there is a winning grace about thee that fain would bid me hope.——" Nay, but who art thou, fair Sir, to venture thus upon our privacy, to tell of names forgotten and unknown, and ope the book of dim antiquity ?"—A stranger, but a friend.

    Come, then, wander awhile with me through old abandoned halls, through lordly chambers and gay terraces, linger awhile within this woody glade, or 'neath the shade of yon sequestered oak ; enter the silent mansions of the dead, think of the gay, the bountiful, the bold, lying in this blank earth ; list to the gladsome power of the village bells, calling the young and old for praise and prayer to yonder chapel, which " like a wild bird's nest, closely lies embowered." Here lies the rustic maiden in her May of youth and beauty fallen; here the brave warrior with his shield of pride and hands upraised in prayer. From the cloudy wreck of time let memory weave afresh bright images, and if for a moment the present is forgotten, and other days come back with recollected music, let us remember, amid this ruin of hoar antiquity, that as the loyal and the brave have passed away, so we shall cease to be.

PARISH OF PRESTBURY.

THE Parish of Prestbury, "the antiquitie, etimologie, and priviledges of which," (to quote the words of the venerable Society of Antiquaries in 1598,) we purpose to consider, presents some most important claims on the attention of the Antiquary, the Naturalist, and the Philosopher, with which we will preface our little sketch.

ITS EXTENT.—The Parish being about forty miles in circumference, and comprising thirty-two townships, with a population amounting nearly to eighty thousand, and containing a venerable Mother Church, with nineteen dependant chapels, (including two which are domestic) in addition to rising fabrics at Woodford and Sutton, which soon to "solemn consecration will be given."

ITS ANTIQUITY.—Prestbury being (as sage Camden hath it) " the most surpassing nursery of ancient gentry," whereof a proud array of splendid ancestry stands here recorded ; and the Parish presenting no shadowy outline of Roman dominion and Saxon grandeur.

ITS FERTILITY.—The lower grounds being bounteous in vegetation, owing to the beneficial rains, and the pasture lands equal to the most lovely spots of our favoured isle.*

ITS SALUBRITY.—When of old we read that " the people had no need of physicians, but the sick man made him a posset, and tied a kerchief on his head and recovered," and now our hale old sires, and the sure chronicle of human mortality, " the village Churchyard," bear witness to the fact.†

ITS INDUSTRY—As tells the busy hum of tongues,

> " And those huge buildings, where incessant noise
> Is made by springs and spindles, girls and boys ;"

and the swarthy denizens of the lower earth, the coal pits, give a lasting evidence of diligence and toil.

With this " avaunt-coureur" of our motives, we proceed :

---

* More rain is said to fall in Cheshire than any where else, excepting the county of Westmoreland.

† Margaret Broadhurst, of Rainow, called " the cricket of the hedge," a former dependant of the Downes', died at the age of 140, and was buried at Prestbury about 1711.

B

PRESTBURY.

The village of Prestbury is beautifully situated on the banks of the Bollin, a river which, rising near Shutlingslow Hill, retains the appearance of a mountain stream in its course through Sutton, till, at Macclesfield, it contributes its waters to the purposes of manufacture, and thence flows on, dark and defiled, till here it seems to have somewhat escaped from the contagion. Leaving Prestbury, it receives the Dean at Wilmslow, and falls into the Mersey near Warburton, after a winding course of twenty miles.

One quiet street, if it deserves the name, constitutes the whole extent of the village. At the south end stands the Hall, " no embattled house with massive keep," fair reader; but a quiet mansion, of modern days, built about fifty years ago, once a village inn, and late the residence of T. Hope, Esq. and afterwards of J. Norbury, Esq. but now untenanted. Some quaint old buildings of other days adorn this peaceful spot, and the north end terminates in a romantic bridge of two arches, over the Bollin; whilst a little above, the grey church tower looks down with solemn majesty, upon its own sweet vale.

Prestbury, although unnoticed in the Doomsday Survey 1088, owing, perhaps, to its devastation by the Norman Invaders, appears from its name to have contained a religious establishment of importance during the Saxon period; and the existence of the ruins of an early Norman Chapel, with the discovery of a Cemetery at Butley in the neighbourhood, in the year 1808, somewhat confirms this idea; which is also supported by its proximity to the supposed Roman road from Condate or Kinderton, near Middlewich, to Rainow and Buxton.

The Church, which has St. Peter for its Patron Saint, is seated at the north end of the village, on a slight eminence above the river, and deserves especial mention, both on account of its architectural excellence, and as being connected in the minds of many, by those thousand threads of association which the memory of the departed always entwine. Here lie, with but perchance a simple stone to mark their resting place, the Leghs, the Downes, the Worths, and many " a gentle knight and fair ladye," whose names long since are swept down the unceasing stream of time; and here, till 1750, floated the proud banners of Crecy and of Agincourt, with other lost memorials of ancient prowess and deeds of arms.

The Church now consists of an ancient tower, (of the date of which there is no evidence, but from the style probably of the fifteenth century) a nave, chancel, and side aisles, formerly terminated in two private chancels; that of the north aisle (which was rebuilt by Charles Legh, of eccentric memory, about 1750, in wretched taste) belonging to the house of Adlington, and still bearing an inscription, under an armorial shield of stained glass in the east window, imploring prayers for the souls of Thomas and Sibilla Legh, " who erected this window 1601."

The chancel of the south aisle, which yet retains its piscina and a portion of the carved oak screen, was founded by the ancient family of the Worths of Titherington. Slight relics of stained glass still exist, but only one monument, ("and that too a memorial needs,") of this proud race exists, an alabaster slab in the wall, containing recumbent figures of a knight and lady, surrounded by an indistinct inscription to the memory of Jasper and Alex Worth, 1572.

In the chancel are also monumental slabs to Sir Edward Warren, 1458, to Reginald Legh, 1482, and formerly a similar memorial to Robert Downes, 1495; but the reforming hand of Charles Legh spared not these relics of antiquity, and

> " Many a sepulchral stone,
> With emblems graven and with footworn epitaph,"

has suffered probably from this invasion.

A few other monuments we shall notice under their respective families. The front of the organ gallery is decorated with the armorial bearings of the proud ones of the Parish, reading a striking lesson of human pride even at the grave.

The west end of the Church is of considerable antiquity, but the general effect of the interior is not improved by the modern taste of the north aisle.

In the crowded churchyard, where many a stout yeoman is at rest, stands a rude building, on which conjecture wastes itself in vain. In 1740, it was fast falling to decay, when Sir William Meredith, of Henbury, stayed its destruction. It now consists of a small nave and chancel, but the west front of the old fabric alone remains. Over a semicircular arch, ornamented with the Chevron and Saxon mouldings, are seven rude figures, in appearance representing our Saviour and his Disciples. Within the arch, was a stone, (now in the interior,) containing figures of the Trinity. We should ascribe it to the early Norman period, as otherwise this church would have been alluded to in Domesday, and have no doubt that it was erected subsequent to the Conquest. The building was used by the Merediths, as a burial place, and is now fitted up for the Sunday School.*

The living is a Vicarage, the heir of Adlington being the Lay Impropriator. Titherington, Upton, Fallibroome and Siddington, pay corn tithes, and those of Capesthorne are attached to that chapel. The Rev. John Rowlls Browne, residing opposite the Church, has been Vicar of the Parish since 1800, and the Rev. J. W. Chaloner, of Adlington, officiates as his Curate. In the Sunday School, 120 children, principally girls, are taught the sacred page of truth. The present population of Prestbury Township is about 500, chiefly agricultural. The Church contains 800 sittings.

---

* The existence of Saxon mouldings is no proof of its being erected prior to the Conqueror, as the early Norman style constantly admits of these.

In 1160, the Manor and Church of Prestbury were granted by Hugh Cyveliok, fifth earl, to the abbey of St. Werburgh in Chester, which enjoyed it with many other benefices till the Dissolution; but the Leghs of Adlington held a lease of the Impropriated Rectory, from 1448.

After the Dissolution, the Manor and Advowson were granted to the Dean and Chapter; from whom, by the summary process of imprisonment, they were extorted by Sir Richard Cotton, in 1547; but in the year 1579 were finally confirmed to the Leghs, in which family they still remain, and a Court Leet and Court Baron are held for the same, twice in the year.

ADLINGTON.

We have now to bring upon the scene, the first of those high families whose names will ever bloom in our memories, when the lengthened scrolls and praise-encumbered stones shall crumble into dust. Adlington, " the spacious and fertile demesne of the Leghs," a goodly tree from which many flourishing branches have sprung, is a Township, containing 1076 inhabitants, situated about five miles from Macclesfield, very rich and fertile, being well watered, and in a great measure included in the Park Grounds. The manor, held in demesne by the Saxon and Norman Earls, seems to have comprised several Townships, which were severed from it soon after the Conquest. Adlington itself came by grant from the Earl to the De Corona's, a family of whom we first hear about 1250. Hence, through four descendants, it passed to Ellen, married to John Legh of Booths, whose younger son, Robert, succeeded to Adlington. The estate then descended through fifteen generations in a direct male line to Charles Legh, who, dying in 1781, without male issue, settled the same on Elizabeth Davenport, wife of John Rowlls, of Kingston, from whom Adlington passed in 1806 to Richard Crosse, Esq., of Preston, whose grandson, now a minor, is the next heir. We have not space to enter on the fortunes of this illustrious house, or to expatiate on their alliance with the Savages, the Venables, the Stanleys, and Worths, and many other names high in the bead roll of fame. We must only glance at two scions of that noble house, Sir Urian and Charles Legh. The former, a fine portrait of whom, with his " Sweet Lady," hangs on the staircase at Adlington, and a copy of which is preserved at Bramhall, was knighted at the taking of Cadiz by the Earl of Essex, in 1596, and is said to have been the original of that beautiful old Spanish ballad, given in Percy's Reliques, which records a fine example of connubial love :—

> " Will you hear a Spanish lady,
> How she woo'd an Englishman."

But we must not mar its beauties by an extract, and refer our readers to the ballad itself. Sir Urian greatly improved the Hall and Park during his residence here.

Charles Legh, Lord of Adlington from 1735 to 1781, ruled his petty kingdom with an iron sceptre. He used to walk about with his favourite dogs and his stout oak cudgel, (as he is represented in a portrait in Adlington Hall,) and chastise the refractory and the drunkard very summarily; all merry makings and wakes were his abhorrence. To his fanciful taste, we are indebted for the *modern improvements* at Adlington, and the *architectural elegance* of the north aisle of Prestbury. Among other traits of his character, it is recorded of him that he was in the habit of beating the bounds of his estate every evening, we conclude to satisfy his vanity, or to expel marauders.

This excellent representative of the feudal times died at Buxton. A mural monument at Prestbury, records his virtues with those of his son.

In the Church at Eccleston, formerly was the following inscription:—

Of your charitie pray for the soul of Thos. Legh,
Of Adlington,
1548.

Adlington Hall, "a stately and commodious house," as the old Chronicler hath it, was entirely remodelled by Charles Legh. It is built in a quadrangular form, the one side of timber and plaister, containing the ancient hall of the time of Elizabeth, a noble room with a handsome organ and galleries of a later date. The principal front, which is of brick, and built about 1740, contains the chapel, the interior of which from the family gallery has a very imposing effect. The approach from the Stockport road is noble, but the spacious stables, also built by Charles Legh, and outbuildings, are rather too prominent. At the rear of the mansion, is a fine sheet of water laid out in the quaint old style, and the soft streamlet of the Dean trills softly through the flowery meads around. Adjoining the high road is the Mill House, a jointure farm of the Leghs; and nearer Hazel Grave, W. Clayton, Esq. has a very pretty villa residence.

The Park, which boasts of many giants of the forest, and is now rearing a nursery of young saplings, is very extensive, and pleasantly varied with avenues and undulations. From a small building on the rising ground, the view of the adjacent hills is very pleasing.

The Gardens reflect great credit on the taste of the present proprietor, having been recently laid out, and a pretty retreat, surrounded by flowery rockwork, overlooks the gay parterre.

The Hall suffered for its loyalty to the Crown, during the Civil wars, having been garrisoned with 150 men, and taken by the Roundheads, after a fortnight's siege, in 1645.

The former Chapel stood in the Park, and originated in a license from William, Bishop of Lichfield and Coventry. It is believed to be a chapel of ease to Prestbury, and to have formerly had a regular minister. The present Chapel is unconsecrated. A Court Leet, and a Court Baron granted 1470, are held twice a year for the Manor, at which debts under 40s. are recoverable.

BIRTLES.

Birtles, a most rich and luxuriant Estate, and ornamented with one of the most elegant villa residences that the county can boast of, lies on the right of the Macclesfield and Knutsford road, about $3\frac{3}{4}$ miles from the former place.

From a Roman urn, which formerly contained burnt bones, found in the grounds, and the numerous tumuli in the neighbourhood, it is conjectured that the road from Condate to Rainow passed through this Township, and the name of Pepper Street, in the immediate vicinity, somewhat confirms this assertion. The manor was held about 1300 by Adam de Astul, who assumed the local name, and this family continued quietly in possession of it for nearly three hundred years, to 1597, when it passed by marriage with Mary Birtles to the Swettenhams, of Swettenham, who made the Hall their residence till 1783, when it became the property of Joseph Fowden, and was by him resold to Robert Hibbert, Esq., whose son now possesses it.

On the Pasture Estate adjacent, in Alderley, the late Mr. Hibbert built an elegant Italian villa, which, for symmetry of proportions and choice of situation, may vie with any in the county. The old Hall, clad in tangled ivy, forms a very picturesque object from the high road, surrounded by many noble monarchs of the forest. The landscape, from the higher grounds, is very pleasing and extensive, and commands rich and unrivalled pasture lands with wild and distant hills.

Whirley Hall, in this Township, a very picturesque old building with gables, and prettily seated in a gentle vale, was long the residence of a collateral branch of the Birtles, as appears from their crest on a pillar yet standing near the Entrance Gates, a lion and birch tree. We are led to believe that some members of the Swettenham family resided here. The stable is old and curious.

In Wanley's Wonders, 1678, we read of Mr. Thomas Birtles living " near unto Maxfield," of extraordinary stature.

The Birtles of Whirley afterwards resided in Macclesfield, and one of the family was mayor of that town in 1630. Elizabeth, the last of the name, married Mr. Stone, Surgeon, grandfather of the present Rector of Spitalfields, in London.

In Prestbury Church, is a handsome monument to the late Mrs. Hibbert, of Birtles, 1817.

The Township of Birtles contains a population of about 60.

Hare Hill, Birtles, is the residence of William Hibbert, Esq.

BUTLEY.

This "spacious Lordship," as Webb hath it, including in its limits part of the Park Grounds of Adlington, separated from Prestbury by the stream of the Bollin, was held at the time of the Domesday Survey, in part by the Saxon Uluric, who probably purchased this favour of retaining his lands by base servility to the invaders, and partly by Robert, son of Hugh Lupus. Butley, before 1250, passed into the hands of the Pigots, Lords of Waverton and Broxton at the Conquest, in which family it continued till about 1560, when after an intermediate sale to the Worths and others, it was purchased by the Leghs, and still continues an appendage of Adlington.

Butley, which is distant from Macclesfield about 2¾ miles, and lies to the left of the Stockport road, could once boast of three goodly seats, the glory of which has long since passed away.

Butley Hall, situated near Prestbury, about 1750 passed from the Watts to the Downes of Shrigley ; in 1790 was purchased by the Leghs ; and is now, by gift from his grandmother, vested in the Rev. John Rowlls Browne, being tenanted by Mrs. Antrobus. Foxwist Hall, now a humble tenement at the confines of Adlington Park ; but with the traces of a double moat existing, was long the residence of the Duncalfes, a family of high degree about 1300, of which a maiden lady residing at Styperson is the representative. Foxwist passed to the Leghs about 1600. There is a stone in Prestbury Churchyard in memory of one of the race, 1720.

Willet Hall, seated near Mottram Park, and now a pretty farm house, passed from the Willets to the Mottersheads, and so to Laurence Wright, Esq. But this Township carries us farther back into remote antiquity, by the discovery in 1808, of a Saxon cemetery, in a field adjoining the Manchester road, consisting of numerous cairns, with a large urn, and a collection of human bones ; and this favours the opinion of Prestbury having been a Saxon religious establishment.

Thomas Newton, who was at the same time a disciple of Esculapius and of the muses, and even as an historian and divine was far beyond his times, was born at Butley, and educated at Macclesfield School under Brownsherd ; whose epitaph from his classic pen still exists. He afterwards practised physic, studied at Oxford, was elected Master of Macclesfield School, and died at his rectory of Little Ilford, in Essex. He was the author of a History of the Saracens, translated Seneca, and was a great protegeé of the Earl of Essex.

Butley contains an increasing population of 900, engaged to some extent in trade, and has a Dissenting place of worship near the river, with a School attached, where 100 children are educated.

BOLLINGTON.

Although the contemplation of the past weaves for us soft and beautiful illusions, unmixed with any of those petty feelings of the present which distract the mind, still it is a painful pleasure, and nourishes the melancholy reflection that the great and good have passed away and are not ; but with those places which only now seem bursting into eminence, hope mingles fair prospects of a glorious future, and so it is with Bollington. This village, not many centuries ago included in the wild domains of a pathless forest, may soon be named high in the scale of our great trading towns. Its early history is very concise. From the neighbouring hill of Kerridge it is conjectured that the Roman road passed through the Township ; and the name of Cold Harbour, between it and Titherington, confirms this idea. It passed with the Manor and Forest of Macclesfield, and at the Swainmote held in 1581, Thomas Grene, Laurence Clarke, and John Taylor, were the Keepers of the Township. The collieries, worked here at a very early period, first brought it into notice ; and within the last few years trade and manufacture have brought it to its present flourishing condition.

The population, in 1811 amounting to 1518, and in 1831 to 2685, now at the lowest computation reaches 3580, and is estimated by some at nearly 6000 ; but in a thickly peopled place like this it is impossible to speak with accuracy. In 1835, a handsome Gothic Church, of the early English style, was erected, at the cost of £4000, containing 750 sittings. A grant was made by the Parliamentary Commissioners, and £50 was presented for the Burial Ground, by the Diocesan Church Building Society. The site was generously given by William Turner, Esq., and the Rev. R. B. Robinson contributed the Books. The Minister then appointed was the Rev. R. King, succeeded by the Rev. W. Daniels, and the Rev. G. Palmer is now the much esteemed Curate.

Adjoining the Churchyard has been erected a neat School House, the upper room of which, fitted up with great taste, is devoted to a Sunday School, giving scriptural instruction to 300 children ; while, in the lower, an Infant School has been very lately opened, at present educating 180, under the ingenious system of Mr. Wilderspin.

The situation of Bollington is very picturesque, and before the huge "steam towers," as Crabbe calls them, marred its beauties, must have been a sweet retreat. The Panorama from the approach to the Viaduct of the Canal, which passes through this Township, is very interesting.

Ingersley Hall, partly in Rainow, the beautiful seat of J. U. Gaskell, Esq., a county magistrate, the descendant of a family resident at Tower Hill, Rainow, as early as 1632, commands a rich prospect of this pretty valley ; the hill which terminates the Kerridge Range, called by the fanciful name of White Nancy, appearing on one side, and farther on the other, the pretty Church of Shrigley, with the summit of the Nab Hill, lately planted.

In Bollington are three Dissenting Chapels and two Schools, in addition to a Romish School and Chapel.

Hollin Hall, in this Township, an interesting old building with gables, was long the residence of a family of the name of Broster, who migrated from Bosley about 1670.

BOLLINGTON CHURCH AND SCHOOL HOUSE

The Greens, of Endon, have also for many centuries been settled here.

Kerridge Hill, lying partly in Rainow, seems to derive its name from Caer, which is an evident allusion to the Roman road, supposed to have swept round the extremity of it. On this hill are several collieries, and large quarries of sandstone, peculiarly adapted for flags or whetting tools, and formerly used for roofing houses. They were of old leased by the Crown to the Corporation of Macclesfield, but were assigned in 1625 to the proprietors of lands in the vicinity. They now belong to Mr. Clayton, who has constructed a tramroad for the conveyance of stone to the canal.

BOSLEY.

The Township of Bosley, which in olden time bore also the name of Lea, probably from a petty stream, lies six miles from Macclesfield on the Leek road, of itself prettily situated, but much indebted for the beauty of its scenery to the romantic banks of the Dane, and the wild fantastic Cloud Hill. Its history is varied and eventful, having been the only Township in the Parish vested in the Crown independent of the local Earldom. The manor, having belonged after the conquest to Hugo Mara and the noble Barons of Montalt, passed in 1327 to Isabel, mother of King Edward III., and continued vested in the Sovereign for 124 years, if we except a temporary grant to the Earl of Salisbury, forfeited at the beheading of his nephew 1394. From King Henry VI. the manor came by grant to the Stanleys in 1454, and afterwards was held by the hero of Flodden, Lord Monteagle, in 1520. From his son, Bosley passed to the Fittons of Gawsworth, about 1540, and is now vested in their successor, the Earl of Harrington, of Elvaston Castle, near Derby. A branch of the Leghs of Adlington, by the name of Macclesfield, said to have been possessed of the manor, and to have exchanged it for the Old Castle and Palace Yard at Macclesfield, to Edward Stafford, Duke of Buckingham, is elsewhere unmentioned, and the Dukes being not historically connected with the neighbourhood, except by the mysterious ruins mentioned in Macclesfield, it appears that this is a mere tradition ; if not, the manor might have been granted to the Leghs and forfeited to the Crown at Stafford's death. So much for conjecture.

The Chapel of Bosley, well situated, but rather too much exposed to the high road, was founded before 1400. The present fabric, erected in 1777, is of brick, with an embattled tower, in appearance about 350 years old. By the exertions of the present Minister, in 1834 the Church was repaired and a new chancel built, the expence being defrayed by a rate, and a grant from the Church Building Society, greatly assisted by voluntary contributions. There are now 500 sittings, of which 110 are free. The Rev. William Sutcliffe, of Oaklands, is the much esteemed Minister. Above the Church, and by the high road, is a peculiarly neat School House, erected in 1839, by private aid and a grant from the National School Society. Here 60 Sunday and 50 daily Scholars study the page of holy writ. Immediately behind the School is a large artificial Reservoir, formed by the Canal Company, covering an area of 120 acres. Its appearance from the hills is very striking, assuming the form of a large Mere, and it is well stocked with fish.

The Township of Bosley contains a population of about 630, and within its limits are silk and cotton mills.

A branch of the Hollinsheds were once settled here, and the names of Chorley, Clowes, and Stonehewer, once graced the list of the stout yeomen of Bosley.

CAPESTHORNE.

Although we confess that our sympathies are engaged " where the dead walls rear their ivy mantles," rather than by the gorgeous palaces of modern days, in a word, that we prefer a Haddon to a Chatsworth; it is a pleasure to see a noble structure rise crowning a fair demesne, and especially when in unison with the architecture of our old English Halls, and such is Capesthorne. But first to trace its history.

From the noble Lords of Aldford, grantees from the Earl, it was held by the Capesthornes, on performance of military service, and thence by marriage passed about 1350 to the Wards; for eight generations Capesthorne was their residence, till about 1570 the Manor was purchased by a colletaral branch of the name, at Monksheath, in Alderley.

After four generations, the sole heiress brought Capesthorne in marriage to Davies Davenport, whose great grandson, the Lord of Woodford and Marton, E. D. Davenport, Esq., here resides. The situation is exquisite, below the peaceful vale of Siddington with a crystal sheet of water, called Reeds Mere, embosomed in the deep foliage beneath. The Park well wooded, and luxuriant with the Christmas holly. The Mansion very recently completed on the site of the ancient Hall, is in the Elizabethan style, with a handsome portico in front, and fitted up internally with splendid elegance. Seen from the water, this glorious pile gleams in lengthened vista through the trees, and looks proudly down upon its dependant vassals.

The Chapel, situated on the right of the Mansion, and dedicated to the Holy Trinity, remains untouched by man's improving hand, with the exception of some slight alterations in the interior. It was built by John Ward, about 1700, and endowed with £400 from the Tithes of the Township, and has since received £600 royal bounty. The yearly value of the Chapelry, in the gift of Mr. Davenport, in 1831 amounted to £76.

The Chapel contains 80 sittings, and service is regularly performed by the Rev. R. H. Heptinstall.

Capesthorne supports by agriculture a population of about 80.

CHELFORD.

This Township, environed on all sides by park scenery and rich wood-lands, is situated about six miles from Macclesfield, on the Knutsford road, the Alderley estate flanking it on one side, and Capesthorne and Withington on another.

The manor was granted by the Earl of Chester to the Despenser and Waverton families, and held under them by the Pigots and Worths, for the yearly render of a pair of gloves on the Feast of All Saints. Robt. Worth granted it to the Abbey of St. Werburgh about 1350, to be held by tenure of a pair of white spurs and a barbed arrow, and by finding a Chaplain to pray for ever in the Chapel of Chelford. After the dissolution it passed to the Dean and Chapter, and thence, 1580, to the Mainwarings of Carincham, from whom it came by sale to a family of the same name, of Peover, whose descendant, Sir Harry Mainwaring, now possesses it, as an appendage of Barnshaw-cum-Goosetrey.

The Chapel, situated on a slight eminence near the high road, owes its foundation to Robert de Worth, 1350, and was rebuilt in 1776; being now a neat but very plain brick building, and of course devoid of interest to the antiquarian. It was endowed with £600 private benefaction, £600 Royal Bounty, and is in the gift of Mr. Dixon. The Rev. John Parker, who died 1795, endowed a School here, with £17 per annum, at which 65 children are educated. The chapel contains 377 sittings, and has an annual stipend of £135. The Rev. G. Granville is the present incumbent.

Astle, in this Township, formerly giving name to a family of the title, of which the Birtles were a branch, is now the seat of John Dixon, Esq. by purchase from Col. Parker, the descendant and successor of the ancient families of Snelson and of Smallwood.

The house, combining comfort and elegance, overlooks the Middlewich road. The Park is rich in beauty of landscape; here groups of solemn oaks, that tuft the swelling mounts; there, extending to the Chapel, a transparent and spacious sheet of water. The grounds altogether are unequalled by any in the neighbourhood.

Chelford contains about 180 inhabitants, and the population is rather on the decline.

FALLYBROOME.

Fallybroome is a name which, save in official documents, seems buried in oblivion, but even this small and now unnoticed Township can claim an honour not to be despised, that of being the first settlement of the knightly and illustrious house of the Fittons, having been granted to them by Hugh Ceveliok, but whether the name then included the whole fee of Bolyn as Wilmslow, &c., seems still a doubtful question. After eight generations of the Fittons, it passed by marriage with the heiress to William Venables, a younger branch of the Kinderton family, and so, in the partition of the family estates, to the Booths, who after three or four generations sold it in severalties. It is last mentioned in 1471, then called Le Fallinge Broome. The Township joins that of Upton, and contains about 20 inhabitants.

HENBURY-CUM-PEXHALL.

To our mind, no object presents a more beautiful succession of pleasing images, than the sight of an English Park; the leafy canopy of gloomy trees, the gently warbling wind, the gurgling brook; the very air breathes silence, and the herds reposing quietly, seem as it were to feel the solemn grandeur of the scene; and this is especially the case in the fair demesne of Henbury, centred in verdant pastures and cheerful shades.

The history of this fine estate can tell of belted knights and courtly esquires. Granted by the Earl to his Constables and Favourites, the Barons of Halton, the Manor passed through the Mainwarings and their successors the Trussels, to Sir John (or Jenkin) Davenport of Wheltrough, about 1350. His descendants allied with the blood of the Venables, the Fittons, and others of high fame, here kept their court for nine generations, till the estate was alienated by Sir Fulk Lucy, (married to Isabella Davenport, and one of the Charlecote family immortalized by Shakespere's witty repartee,) to Sir William Meredith, of Devon, in 1670. From his grandson, it passed by sale to J. B. Jodrell, Esq., in 1779, from whose son, (possessor also of Taxall Manor with its rich fir plantations,) it was purchased by John Ryle, Esq., late M.P. for Macclesfield, descended from a family settled as early as 1500, in Styall, and lying buried in a Chapel formerly of their own, at Wilmslow Church. To Mr. Ryle, the flourishing institutions of Macclesfield are greatly indebted, and no gentleman stands higher in the estimation of high and low. The Hall is a handsome modern residence, much improved by Mr. Ryle.

Henbury, situated between Thornycroft and Birtles, three miles from Macclesfield, on the left of the Knutsford road, nourishes with the Hamlet, Pexhall, a population of about 414.

LYME HANDLEY.

The storied arras, source of fond delight,
With old achievement charms the wildered sight;
And still with Heraldry's rich hues imprest,
On the dim window glows the pictured crest.

There are many to whom the claims of birth may seem ideal, genealogies tedious, and gentility not of the blood but of the individual; but few can gaze on the silent magnificence of a Baronial Hall, the stern bright images of faded tapestry, the antique workmanship and quaint devices, the marble effigies, the haunted chambers,—few can listen to its fairy legends and romantic lays, without revering the race of the brave, and honouring the memory of the past. Who can enter the halls of Lyme without a thought of the heroes who fell in England's brightest days?

Lyme Handley, tenanted of old by the merry outlaws of the wood, and untrodden save by the solitary step of the hardy forester, was granted by the Black Prince, in 1398, to Sir Piers Legh, of Macclesfield, as a guerdon for the services of his father-in-law, Sir Thomas Danyers, in the field of Crecy. This Sir Piers was a younger son of Robert Legh, of Adlington, and having " left not King Richard in his troubles," sealed his loyalty to the Plantagenets by his death at Chester, having been beheaded by the Duke of Lancaster. His head was affixed to the East Gate of the City, but his bones rest in the Chapel at Macclesfield ;

" Where near this brave knight his son too lies entombed,"

Sir Peter Legh, who died at Paris of wounds received in the glorious victory of Agincourt. In 1630, another laurel was added to this race of stately Cavaliers, by alliance with Lettice, eighth in descent from the hero of Froissart, Sir Hugh Calveley, " a warrior, (quoth old Camden,) of feet and hands, who would feed as much as three men, and fight as much as ten men." The direct male line terminated, after thirteen generations, in 1797, in T. P. Legh, Esq., in whose veins flowed the blood of the Savages and the Gerards. Thomas Legh, Esq., late M.P. for Newton, is the present possessor.

To do justice to such a noble pile as Lyme Hall, would be impossible. We could almost be content to leave it with the quaint, but glowing description by Webb ; "a stately seat, with the large and spacious park, richly stored with red and fallow deer, and with all other fitness for Lordly delights."

The Hall bursts suddenly upon the eye on descending the hill at the approach from the Shrigley side, in gloomy majesty, breathing an air of silence and repose. But take a nearer survey of this splendid building. The south and west fronts are in the Palladian style, from a design by Leoni; and some portions of the Mansion were erected by Sir Peter Legh, about 1600; enter through the cloistered quadrangle ; ascend this massive flight of steps ; the noble Hall, the scene of many a long carouse, " where mirth and music told the dirge of care," hung with dark portraits of grim warriors and modern gallants, old armour too, which would fain boast of the field of Crecy. Mount this handsome staircase, paying a just tribute to some choice portraits of Cheshire worthies. The Drawing Room ! What a dim religious light streams softly through that exquisitely stained window. The ceiling, too, how gorgeous with gold ; pass through a pretty summer room with little azure tinctured grotesques on old china, and a view of the old Hall, seemingly of the world before perspective, over the chimney piece, to the large

Dining Room. Look out upon this noble conservatory; pause to admire the master work of Gibbons, which surmounts the fire place;—but we shall ramble too far. With the passing mention of an Elizabethan gallery, 124 feet in length, which forms part of the old building; a wainscotted room ornamented with chef d'euvres of Gibbon's carving, rivalling his Chatsworth labours, and a tapestried one, of Miss Legh's fair handiwork; we must conclude this sketch with the passing mention, that of course, two beds are especially appropriated to the Black Prince and Mary Queen of Scots.

The paintiugs are numerous, but without any of very superior eminence. Among the portraits, we notice one by Kneller, of Admiral Legh, and likenesses of Sir Peter Legh, and James Earl of Derby. The house is enriched with objects of vertū, selected by the present possessor, who is said to have explored every country in Europe, attired in the national costumes.

The Chapel, which is of the Ionic order, lies in mournful desolation. There are no parterres or pleasure grounds, as at Chatsworth; but perhaps they would not be strictly in unison with the ancient grandeur of the Mansion, and the wildness of the situation.

The Park, containing 1000 Cheshire acres, is bleak and desolate, but admits of rich and varied prospects, especially from a ruined building called Lyme Cage. Here is a herd of wild cattle, mentioned by Leland, and by the natives called indigenous, but certainly found only at Chillingham Castle, and Gisburne Park, in Yorkshire, and some also domesticated at Vale Royal. They are white with red ears, and remove their quarters from the hills to the valley with the change of weather. A curious custom, now extinct, of which a mention occurs in a note to the Lady of the Lake, prevailed here. The deer were driven through a sheet of water, and the company "stood with swords drawn to have a cut at the stag at his coming out of the water."

> Twice that day, from shore to shore,
> The gallant stag swam stoutly o'er.

The Earl of Essex witnessed this hazardous exploit. Of the feat, also practised at Adlington, there is a print by Vivares.

Joshua Watson, Keeper 64 years, buried at Disley, and immortalized by a portrait at the Hall, directed these sports with great success.

The Manor of Norbury, with the Patronage of Disley, is in the gift of Mr. Legh.

Lyme Handley, assuming its first name from its situation on the limes or borders of the County, is situated above the quiet and romantic Village of Disley. The Hall and Grounds lie to the right of the Manchester and Buxton Road, and extend to Taxal and Whaley Moor, towards which district is the hamlet of Hanley strictly so called. The Township is situated about seven miles from Macclesfield, and contains 200 inhabitants.

At one of the gates of Lyme Park, near a solitary hut, and in a situation which overlooks the wild country of Taxall, on the one side, and commands a most extensive view on the East, with the sea in the distant horizon, are two circular pillars, called the Bow Stone, hewn with rude blocks, but having a fillet traced round the top of each, and slight vestiges of other ornaments.

Whether these were forest boundary stones, (as is assumed from the existence of similar ones on Longside Hill, in Whaley, and at Ludworth, but which the situation surely disapproves, whether plague stones (as those at Eyam,) which the existence of the adjacent gravestones corroborates, but which is rendered unlikely by their unfinished appearance, remains a mystery which time may never unravel.

Near this spot are said to be several gravestones, three of which we could only discover. Tradition deems them to be those of persons who died from the plague, which raged in Congleton, and slightly in Macclesfield, in 1603 and 1641; and at Chester also in 1648. Others would suppose them to be victims of the Puritans; but the situation is too retired, and we hear of no military operations in the neighbourhood, (except the capture of Chester in 1646,) from the taking of Adlington, 1645, to July, 1648, when a party of Royalists from Whaley Bridge, made an incursion into the chamber of the Forest.

We subjoin the Epitaphs; immediately above Bow Stone, but hardly legible,

Robert Blakewell,
1646

And on the other side of the hill,

John Hampson and his wife
and three children deed this life
1646
Think not strange our bones ly here
Thine may ly thou knowest not where
1646.

MARTON.

The Township of Marton, or Meretune, situated in a low and rather uninteresting part of the Parish, on the Manchester and Birmingham road, and containing an agricultural population of 365, derives its name from a large mere near the Hall, now dwindled into a mill pool. Held at the Conquest by the Saxon Godfric, for probably base service to the Invaders, it passed with his fourth descendant to Gilbert Venables, grandson of the first Baron of Kinderton. His granddaughter brought it in 1176, to Richard Dauneport, for the annual service of six barbed arrows; and for 664 years Marton has formed one of the bright gems of this princely heritage; a moiety of it severed in 1733, having been repurchased in 1760.

The Hall which graced this ancient manor, now occupied by a farmer, is a plain timber mansion, terminating in gables, on the left of the Congleton and Wilmslow road, with no other vestiges of its knightly lords, except some pikes suspended in the Hall, and the Davenport arms curiously carved in a wainscotted room.

The Chapel lying on the opposite side of the road, a little beyond, must arrest the eye of every traveller, especially as contrasted with the Collegiate pile of Astbury, on the same route.

The fabric, excepting the spire and the brick chancel, is probably of the date of the foundation of the Chantry, 1343, and a most rude and curious specimen of timber work. Some fragments of stained glass remain in the chancel and west end windows, in appearance representing the beheading of John the Baptist and the armorial bearings of the Davenports and Siddingtons. The side aisles are separated from the nave by rude timber beams. The interior is very plain, but

> "Admonitory texts inscribe the walls,
> Each in its ornamental scroll enclosed."

A singing gallery was erected in 1813, and the chapel holds about 300 persons. There are Sunday and day Schools in the village, at which 40 children are educated. In the Churchyard, which is particularly neat, but too much exposed to the high road, repose near the porch, two recumbent figures, now mutilated by the hand of time, said to represent Sir John Davenport, fonnder of this chantry, and his son Vivian. The Chapelry, including a part of Lower Withington, was endowed with £200 private benefaction and £400 Royal bounty, the yearly value being about £48. It is in the gift of Mr. Davenport, and the Rev. John Darcey for 34 years has been the Incumbent.

MOTTRAM ANDREW.

In those goodly days, when districts now profaned by unsightly edifices, which tell a melancholy tale of human industry indeed, but also of human woe; when districts now teeming with swarming crowds of the "unwashed, unkempt, unhurt," reared the proud monarch of the wild to heaven, and nursed the merrie company of Robin Hood, there existed many high and honourable offices attached to families in this neighbourhood, which now only exist in name, or shine with diminished lustre. Of these, that of Hereditary Master Forester, held after the Conquest by the Suttons, and from them by the Davenports from 1210 to the present time, will be noticed hereafter, and the stewardship, vested in the Stanley family, will require a distinct mention.

The office of "Le Gaolar," or Bailiff of the Forest, at present under consideration, though to modern ears, a post of emolument more than of dignity, was nevertheless in those days one of considerable honour, and consisted in executing processes, carrying the mace, receiving the rents of the King, and in many other offices of trust. In the enjoyment of this dignity, continued from before 1350 to 1420, a family who took their local name from Mottram, and held their Manor, from an early period.

Mottram retained after the Conquest by a Saxon Gamel, passed about 1360, by Marriage with Agnes Mottram, to David Calvely, of Lea, and after continuing in that family for nine generations, in 1636 was vested by purchase in the fourth son of William Booth, of Dunham Massey. From this family, who resided here from 1667 to 1738, the Manor passed to the Wrights of Offerton, whose third descendant, Laurence Wright, Esq. succeeded in 1799, and is the present possessor.

After this somewhat tedious account, we will only mention that about 1650 the Mottersheads, a family now extinct, possessed the Higher and Lower House, and that Lea Hall, in the Township, now let to a farmer named Goodyer, belonged to a branch of the Masseys of Dunham, whose descendant still holds the lands annexed to it. The office of Bailiff passed by forfeiture from the Mottrams, in 1420, to the Savages, and thence to the Cholmondeleys, who now enjoy it, but with its privileges much impaired.

Mottram Hall, seated at the foot of a slight declivity, is an elegant modern residence. The Park, which skirts the Wilmslow road, and reaches nearly to the bridge over the Bollin, near Newton, is extensive, and the house well shrouded in trees. The prospect includes the open country beyond Woodford, with the Alderley and Lyme hills.

On Mottram Common, near a cross erected by Mr. Wright in 1833, is a day school, but the poor of this district stand very much in want of spiritual instruction, and we look forward to the time when a population of more than 400 may hear

> "Their own Sabbath bell's harmonious chime,
> Float on the breeze."

It is said that a Chapel once existed at Mottram, and that a few lonely gravestones still mark the spot; but this seems improbable, as not the slightest mention of it occurs as early as 1669, and possibly the stones, if existing, may be relics of the plague. *There are ab.t 20 stones, dated f.m 1701 to*

The Savages held lands here with a place called Le Halle Howse, in virtue of their office; and here the Archbishop resided for some years.

The Cemetery of the Wrights, (who are also Lords of Offerton,) is at St. Peter's Church, at Stockport, which is in the gift of the family, having been built by William Wright, in 1768. The Rev. Henry Wright, (heir of the Mottram estates, and nephew of the present possessor,) is the present Minister.

NEWTON.

Newton, pleasantly situated about five miles from Macclesfield, between the rivers Dean and Bollin, was probably once annexed to Butley, but held distinctly as early as 1200 by Robert Hyde of Hyde; whose grandson alienated it to Thomas Davenport, and his daughter Sybilla brought it in marriage to Thomas Newton, in 1302. The Newtons, of whom was the eminent scholar mentioned in the account of Butley, and who inherited Pownall by marriage with Ellen Fitton 1496, held this manor for ten generations, till it passed by marriage to the Mainwarings of Hawthorne Hall, and so by purchase to the Leghs of Adlington, in whom it is now vested.

Newton Chapel, which was probably later than 1530 considered domestic, was included by Webbe, 1631, and Leycester, 1670, among the chapels dependant upon Prestbury, and had a warden appointed about the latter time. In 1722 it lay "ruined," and now there remains only a yew tree's shade, where perhaps the rude forefathers of the hamlet sleep unknown and forgotten.

Newton Hall, seated near the Bollin, is now a neat farm house, occupied by a family of the name of Lane.

The Township contains an agricultural population of about 80.

POYNTON.

The lover of nature may well breathe a sigh over the ruin of her fairest spots in these our days of improvement. The country will soon cease to exist, the honest pride in tilling the land which our fathers inherited, and guarding the elm which they planted, is now no more,—the coal wharf, or the hateful railroad, pollutes the groves,

> " Where the rude axe with heaved stroke,
> Was never heard the Nymphs to daunt,
> Or fright them from their hallowed haunt."

Could the proud Barons of Stockport visit again their fair demesnes, they would indeed rejoice that their name had passed away, ere the existence of such scenes as this.

Poynton, although unnoticed in Domesday, was, by an early grant of the Earl, assigned to the Poutrells, under whom it was first held about 1230, by the Barons of Stockport.

Thence, after four generations, the Manor passed about 1369, by marriage with Cicely de Eton, of Stockport, to Sir Edward Warren, lineally descended from the Earls of that name.

This worshipful house, connected at various times in marriage with the Leghs, Stanleys, Fittons, and other knightly families, continued to enjoy the Manor of Poynton, (by a yearly tender of a sparrow hawk to the King,) and that of Stockport, for sixteen generations, till the death of Sir George Warren, K.B. 1801, when the estates devolved to his daughter, married to Lord Bulkeley, and on the extinction of that family and title, to Lord Vernon, Baron of Kinderton, in 1837, through his alliance with the daughter of Sir John B. Warren, of Caunton,

Nottinghamshire, descended from a collateral branch, which was separated from the parent stock about 1470. George John, the present Lord Vernon, born in 1803, assumed the surname and arms of Warren, but has never made Poynton a place of residence, and is now, we believe, residing at Nice.

The ancient and fair old seat of the Warrens, built about 1550, did not survive the ruin of its princely lands, but was removed by Sir George Warren to give way to a handsome Mansion of the Ionic order, seated in a Park which still retains some venerable oaks, and is ornamented by a beautiful sheet of water, now environed by coal wharfs.

> " Such outrage done to nature as may compel
> The indignant power to justify herself."

The house is approached from the entrance lodge, on the Manchester road, by an elegant bridge. The vein of coal was accidentally discovered in the time of Sir George Warren, by some workmen sinking a well for a tenant, and now proves a great source of wealth, though certainly not of improvement to the estate.

The colliers, amounting in this and the adjacent works to 1900, had an altercation with Mr. Ashworth, the Agent, last year, which seemed, for a time, to threaten a serious outbreak. The Hall is tenanted by the Misses Garratt, and the Park is a ley for cattle. The Chapel, said to have been once endowed with the tithes of Poynton and Woodford, dates its origin from Nicholas de Eaton, 1310. In 1831 it was valued at £85 per annum, having received £800 Royal Bounty. The site of the old Chapel was in the Park, at a massive building now called the Towers, and the churchyard is we believe still enclosed. The present fabric was erected by Sir G. Warren, in 1789 ; a new chancel of brick is just finished, but the general appearance of the exterior is not striking. The interior, containing two small galleries, is neat, and contains a painted chancel window. In a pretty gothic school house near the Park, erected by Lady Bulkeley, more than 300 children receive a scriptural education, under the able superintendence of the respected Curate and the Misses Garratt.

The Chapel has now accomodation for nearly 400, and the patronage is vested in Lord Vernon. The Rev. R. Litler is the present Minister, having been appointed in 1832, a man most indefatigable in attending to the spiritual welfare of this increasing population. A Cemetery has lately been enclosed, and a license for burials will be soon obtained. The present population of Poynton is not less than 900.

NORTH RODE.

The Township of North Rode, lying near the banks of the Dane, rising in the Forest, and which here " a crystal liquid brook," afterwards somewhat loses its purity by the smoke of Congleton, and after flowing by the ancient seats of Davenport and Shipbrooke, falls into the Weaver at Northwich, after a swift course of twenty-two miles. The banks of this stream are enriched with deep woods which, when the glowing sunset tints their autumn foliage, produce an effect worthy of the pencil of Turner. North Rode adjoining Bosley, and with the striking summit of the Cloud in view, lies about $4\frac{1}{2}$ miles from Macclesfield, on the Leek road. The Manor, held before the Conquest by the Saxon Ranulph, passed through Bigot and his descendants, the Aldfords, to their successors the Ardernes, 1210, under whom it was held by the Mainwarings of Warincham and the Trussels for eight generations, till in 1500, John Vere, 15th Earl of Oxford, by marriage with Elizabeth Trussel, succeeded to the Manor, and from him having passed in 1578 to Sir Christopher Hatton, it was purchased by Sir Randolph Crewe in 1610, and finally came into the possession of John Smith Daintry, Esq. a few years ago.

The Mansion, lying in a retired position on the Leek road, is the present residence of Thomas Daintry, Esq. Crumwell, Brammall Hill, and Rode Green, mentioned as the Forest boundaries, are in this Township. The land, which is indifferent, supports an agricultural population of about 250 inhabitants.

SIDDINGTON.

The " soft quiet hamlet" of Siddington, which bids fair to rival in the beauty of its rich scenery even the more favoured nooks of the South, lies a little to the right of the Congleton and Wilmslow road, at the distance of five miles from Macclesfield. The spot is indeed enchanting, the picturesque half-timbered chapel, seated on a gentle eminence, with its neat School House, and rude memorials of its village worthies, looking down upon the ancient Hall, which, with rude beams of timber and finished gables, is seated in a gentle valley, hard by " a silver brawling stream," with here and there some clustered cottages and fields of brightest green.

Siddington, held in the same manner as North Rode by Bigot and his successors the Ardernes, was granted about 1350 to the Sydingtons, a branch of the Davenport family, as appears from their armorial bearings, and from the latter holding estates here as early as 1250. The manor then passed, about 1500, by marriage to the Fittons of Gawsworth, who possessed it for six generations by the render of a red rose yearly till the extinction of the family, when it was purchased by the Wards of Capesthorne, and from them has descended to E. D. Davenport, Esq. The present population is 480.

The Chapel, a brick and plaister edifice, is of probably a very much earlier period than 1633, the date which appears carved on the pulpit. A richly carved oak screen, formerly painted and gilt, separates the nave from the chancel, and some curious carving has at some time existed in front of the seats. The pews, excepting that of the Thornycroft family and the Clergyman's, lie within the chancel. The Chapel contains accommodation for 283, and is very well attended under the able ministry of the Rev. R. H. Heptinstall, appointed in 1829. The annual income is £106. The School was founded by John Foden in 1710, and endowed with £8 per annum. The present neat building, attached to the churchyard, was erected about 1825 by Mr. Davenport, when Mr. Bromley was Minister. The number of children instructed is 110, a fact which speaks highly for the management of it. The Chapelry, in the patronage of Mr. Davenport, was endowed with £425, the benefaction of John Foden, and £400, Royal Bounty.

In this Township stands Thornycroft Hall, another noble Mansion of a time honoured race. The house, an elegant structure of modern days, looks down upon a placid Mere, ornamented with verdant foliage of fine old trees, and the grounds are beautifully carpeted with nature's velvet mantle. The road from Macclesfield to Siddington skirts the Park.

The late Mr. Thornycroft, a gentleman of the most bland and courteous manners, whose virtues are fresh in our memories, greatly improved the appearance of the grounds, which are now very beautifully laid out.

Henshaw Hall, situated between Thornycroft and the village of Siddington, and now a farm house, was united to Thornycroft by marriage of the families in 1712.

The Thornycrofts possessed this estate about 1300, by marriage with the Sydingtons, and continued in succession for sixteen generations, till the death of Edward Thornycroft, Esq. in 1817, when the estates passed to the Rev. Charles Mytton, of Eccleston, who assumed the name of Thornycroft, and his son is the present possessor. The two surviving sisters of Edward Thornycroft, Esq. reside at that fine old timbered building, Little Moreton Hall, in Astbury Parish.

In Gawsworth Church, are memorials of Anne and Edward Thornycroft, 1712 and 1726; Mary, their daughter, 1721; Henshaw and Mary Thornycroft, 1780 and 1774; Edward Thornycroft, 1817; Mary, his first wife, 1807; Anne, 2nd wife, Viscountess of Barrington, 1816. John Thornycroft, of Milcomb, Oxfordshire, and Stockwell, created a Baronet in 1701, was descended from this family. The title is now extinct.

TYTHERINGTON.

The Township of Tytherington, situated about a mile from Macclesfield, beside the Stockport road, and containing a population of 450, lies too much in the vicinity of a large manufacturing town, to present many attractions to the admirer of nature, but yet comprises some rich pastures, and pleasing undulations, especially towards the Bollin, which forms the boundary between it and Upton. It was held as a dependancy of the Earl's Manor of Macclesfield, as early as 1258, by the Tideringtons, (the possessors also of large estates in Wervin,) for three generations, and about 1340 passed by marriage to the Worths, originally of the Township of that name. This ancient family, at times ennobled by the alliance of the Davenports and the Vernons, continued lords of this fair demesne for fifteen generations, till the Manor passed in 1695 to Samuel Heath, of Dublin, and after having changed hands seven times in 74 years, came by marriage with Anne Acton, in 1769, to W. Brooksbank; (two sons dying without issue,) his daughter since deceased, brought it in marriage to Sir Edward Stracey, of Rackheath Hall, Norfolk.

The old Manor House, now occupied by a respectable farmer of the name of Mason, lies retired from the high road near the footpath to Prestbury. It yet retains the appearance of having been a seat of importance in the olden time, and the lands attached are fertile and contain some valuable timber.

Higher Beach House, long the residence of Mr. Brooksbank, is seated on an eminence rising from the Bollin, and commands a pleasing prospect of the fertile valley, being well shrouded from the town. The mansion is commodious, but seldom occupied by Sir E. Stracey.

On the right of the high road stands the handsome residence of Wm. Brocklehurst, Esq. prettily environed with rising plantations, and opening a rich prospect of the Kerridge Hills.

UPTON.

Upton, situated about a mile and a half from Macclesfield, on the Prestbury road, and now containing about 80 inhabitants, is almost the only township in this Parish on which early history is silent. It was included in the limits of the Forest, and we have reason to believe that a family existed here for many years, bearing the local name. The Stapeltons however, a branch of a knightly family in Yorkshire, settled here about 1500, and were succeeded in 1670 by the Darceys and Booths, from whom the estate passed by purchase to John Ward, in 1740, and so to his descendant, Davies Davenport, who disposed of the Manor to John Ryle, Esq., of Henbury. Upton Hall, mentioned in 1621 as "a fair brick house, built of late years by Mr. Stapelton," was situated to the right of the road, on an eminence commanding a fine view of the vale of Prestbury, and with a deep wood in the dingle below. It was of late years taken down by Mr. Ryle, and a farm house built near its site. In a pleasant avenue retired from the road, is a small Mansion belonging to Mr. Beck, and opposite Upton Hall, a new house has lately been erected by Mr. Norbury, formerly of Prestbury.

On the Macclesfield side of the Township, E. Hall, Esq. has built a pretty villa residence, seated on an eminence and entirely shut out from the unsightly buildings of the town, by the Westbrook woods.

Between Upton and Fallibroome, by the side of the road, stands a rude relic of other days, a cylindrical stone with a fillet traced upon it, and supposed to be a boundary cross.

OLD WITHINGTON.

It is a striking fact connected with the history of our neighbourhood, that towards the close of the last century, many rich and goodly heritages either fell to distant branches of the ancient stock, or passed to strangers. It would seem as if a new epoch was to arise with the nineteenth century, and that our forefathers foresaw the utter ruin of our venerable customs and old domestic morals. But with the Manor of Old Withington, the case is otherwise; for nearly six hundred years a family, ennobled not more by the glory of ancestry than by the true pride of virtue, has here been settled, and still forms a connecting link between the memory of the past and the hopes of the future.

The Baskervilles, a name conjuring up splendid visions of the mighty emperors of the west, and mighty dukes and kings, their noble ancestors, are directly traced from William Earl of Warenne, located in England after the Conquest.

The principal settlement of this royal race was at Erdesley, in Herefordshire, and from this family, (gracing the roll of Battel Abbey, and for centuries champions of the Kings of England,) we are inclined to derive the house of Withington. The Manor originally connected with Chelford, and held in part by the Pigots and Worths, seems soon after the Conquest to have been added by grant from the Earl to the princly estates of the Aldfords, and was held under them by the Cliftons of Staffordshire, of whom some mention occurs in the wars, but otherwise unconnected with Cheshire. This family granted the manor to Oliver Fitton, (who retained his moiety for a very short time,) and Sir John Baskerville, probably a younger son of the third knight of Erdesley. From him in a splendid descent of sixteen generations, the estates have been handed down to John Baskervyle Glegg, Esq. whose grandfather assumed the name of Glegg, on his alliance with the heiress of Gayton, in Wirrall.

The elegant mansion which graces this fair demesne is seated in an extensive park, abounding "with bowery walks and coverts close, with vistas open and with alleys green." A noble avenue forms an approach from the Middlewich Road. The estate is luxuriant and very excellently cultivated. The Gleggs are Lords of the Manors of Gayton and Pensby, and inherit large estates in Blackden (by alliance with the Kinseys,) and Dodleston.

The Township lies at the extremity of the Hundred adjoining Peover, is situated about eight miles from Macclesfield, and contains an agricultural population of more than 200.

LOWER WITHINGTON.

This Township, which lies west of the former, but is of far greater extent, was granted by Earl Randle Blundeville about 1200, on tender of a pair of gilt spurs, to Robert Salmon, the ancestor of the families of that name in Hatherton and Nantwich. Moieties of the manor were afterwards settled about 1300 on the Davenports and Meres, the latter of whom granted their share to the Mainwarings of Peover about 1388. The manor is now by purchase from Thomas Parker, Esq. the property of J. B. Glegg, Esq.

Wheltrough Hall, an ancient timber mansion, now tenanted by a respectable farmer of the name of Massey, was about 1340 the seat of an illustrious branch of the Davenports, the founder of the Bramhall, Woodford and Henbury families. The Davenports were settled here quietly for twelve generations till 1680, and since that period the hall has passed to the Hollinsheads, Brookes, and Parkers, and is now vested in Mr. Glegg.

Wheltrough, now a pretty retired farm house and occupied by Mr. Massey, forms a very picturesque object from Tunsted Hill immediately above it. This conical summit, *supposed* from its name to be the site of an ancient hamlet, is now planted with firs, and commands a prospect over

> " hill and dale, and wood and lawn,
> And verdant fields and darkening heath between,
> And villages embosomed soft in trees."

From this height 34 churches are visible.

In Lower Withington, which has 584 inhabitants, is a school towards which the late Mr. Boden of Macclesfield bequeathed £480.

WOODFORD.

To the imaginative mind every object hath its interest, every spot its associations; for instance in the solitary stone, the last memorial of Fotheringay, it can trace the whole of that affecting scene which closed Queen Mary's ill-fated career, and the ruined walls of Kenilworth it can people with fair ladies and courtly cavaliers, and picture the humbled Amy Robsart kneeling at the feet of proud Queen Bess. Thus even the ruined hall of Woodford tells

> " Of lovers' slights, of ladies' charms,
> Of witches' spells, of warriors' arms."

But to our subject :

Woodford, situate at the extremity of the Parish, and separated from Wilmslow by the river Dean, is first mentioned about 1180 among the estates of Sir John Arderne, Grantee of twenty Townships from the sixth Earl of Chester.

About 1239 the Manor passed to the noble family of the Stockports, and, after four generations, in 1370 to their heir John Warren, who again conveyed it to Sir Jenkin Davenport. His son Nicholas coming into possession was the ancestor of this distinguished branch, who have allied themselves with the Savages and other ladies of high degree, and have possessed the Manor for sixteen generations; E. D. Davenport, Esq. being the present proprietor.

On the summit of the hill, above the Dean, a neat structure of brick is rising as a Chapel of Ease to Prestbury. It will contain 250 sittings, and a portion of the building will be devoted to a Sunday School, of which the Township is now destitute only containing one Calvinistic place of education. The patronage of it will be vested in Mr. Davenport, the possessor of the land. The Earl of Harrington also inherits property in this Township. In a retired situation near the Chapel are the old and new Halls, both now occupied by farmers; the former is in a miserable condition, and the timber beams seem almost bursting from their position. The new Hall, however, bearing on a stone the initials, W. D., 1630, and constructed of brick, is tenanted by a highly respectable farmer of the name of Armstrong.

The population of Woodford now amounts to 423.

Dean Water, the residence of James Andrew, Esq. is a handsome residence on the banks of the brook bearing that name.

WORTH.

The Township of Worth, a name now more generally associated with those collieries which have marred the face of nature in this charming district, than with records of olden times, yet gave name to a family, as we have seen in our notice of Titherington, of no mean importance.

The first historical mention of this family occurs in 1288, when Henry Worth held a subordinate Forestership in right of a tenement in Upton called the Ratonesfield. The Worths were succeeded in this Township by the Hulmes their descendants in the female line, and thence the estate passed by marriage with the heiress Agnes to Roger Downes in 1384. The Lords of Shrigley held Worth as an appendage to their goodly heritage for 308 years, till it was united to Poynton (with which it was originally connected) in 1792 by the purchase of Sir George Warren. The will of Geoffrey Downes in 1492 speaks of their own place at Worth or at Shrigley, as if Worth Hall was an occasional residence of the family.

The Township, now vested in the hands of Lord Vernon, nourishes a population of more than 500, chiefly employed in the collieries.

MACCLESFIELD.

In the cursory view we are taking, we have neither time nor ability to dwell at length on the fortunes of a place, which from being a petty market town, as it is described in 1790, has risen to such a scale of consequence, as to be able to compete with most trading towns in the kingdom. In order the more effectually to condense our information, we propose to offer a concise summary of the most important events connected with the Borough, and then to touch slightly on other topics of consequence which may suggest themselves.

Macclesfield, or Maxfield, the etymology of which is unknown, unless (as some affect,) the name be derived from the original settler, appears from a lengthened notice in Domesday, to have been the seat of the Saxon Earl's Court, and after the Conquest to have been held in demesne by the Norman Earls, several minor vills in the Hundred being dependant on it. About 1100 the place was fortified, and the Park, previously vested in the Davenports, was reunited to the Manor in 1220. Since the extinction of the local Earldom, the Manor has been held by the crown.

Macclesfield was made a free burgh by Earl Randle, probably about 1200, and received additional charters from Prince Edward Earl of Chester in 1261, from Queen Elizabeth in 1564, and from Charles II. in 1678.

The early history of manufacturing towns is generally devoid of interest, yet the Macclesfield men always "demeaned themselves right valiantly in their undertakings," as Fuller hath it; and Richard II. was attended by 2000 Cheshire archers, all having Bouch of Court and Sixpence a day. At the battles of Shrewsbury and Bloreheath, many a Cheshire knight "foremost fighting fell," and tradition tells of the slaughter of Sir John Savage and the Burgesses of Macclesfield at Bosworth, ranged on the side of Richmond and victory; certain it is that in 1513 the fatal field of Flodden numbered Sir Edmund Savage, Mayor, and many noble citizens among the slain. In 1544, William Davenport, Edward Warren, and Edmund Savage were knighted at Leith, for services in Scotland. In 1552 the Free Grammar School was founded by King Edward VI. Thence Macclesfield floated quietly down the stream of time, undisturbed save by the threatenings of the Spanish Armada, towards the defeat of which Thomas Legh and Randall Davenport were contributors, till in 1642 the tide of civil commotion reached this quiet spot. In that year, Colonel Legh of Adlington attempted to seize the town for King Charles, but was defeated by Mr. Mainwaring, who plundered Adlington, and that Hall was taken in 1644. It may be interesting to note the part which the families of the neighbourhood took in these unhappy commotions. Colonel Booth of Mottram greatly aided the Parliament in the blockade of Chester, 1646, and Laurence Downes of Shrigley was Lieutenant Colonel of Bradshaw's regiment at Worcester. Amongst the sufferers in defence of the monarchy, we notice Thomas Legh of Adlington, Maisterson of Woodford, Wood of Poynton, Piggot of Butley, Pickford, Shirt, and Watts, of Adlington, who compounded for their estates. During the Commonwealth, General Fairfax was entertained at Macclesfield, " at a sumptuous civic entertainment" which cost 1s. 3d. In 1659, Colonel Booth (who had changed sides,) and Laurence Wright assisted the rising of Sir George Booth. But we have dwelt too long on this unhappy period. In 1603 and 1646 the plague, which nearly depopulated Congleton, ravaged Macclesfield, but in a less degree ; and in 1668 an entry in the register mentions a subscription of £5 5s. to the poor in London suffering from the fire. A dreadful hurricane occurred in the neighbourhood in 1662. From this period, the town continued quietly engaged with its prosperous button trade, till the visit of the bonny Prince Charlie in 1745, who established his head quarters here ; the unfortunate Prince was attired in a plaid, and wore a blue bonnet with the white rose. From this time, the history of Macclesfield is strictly local. With the exception of the Market Place being enlarged in 1774, and the transmission of the London mail through the place in 1786, we have now to speak only of civil disturbances, which occurred in 1786; again in 1800, when seizure of flour, &c. took place, and during the Manchester riots in 1819. The Corporation in 1797 subscribed £100 towards the war, and in 1802 the freedom of the borough was presented to Prince William Frederick of Gloucester, and the Hon. J. Abercromby. In 1815, £542 was subscribed for the widows of the heroes of Waterloo, and in 1832 the place was enlivened by a visit from our gracious sovereign on her way to Chatsworth. And with this auspicious event we will close our rather tedious account of the *local annales* of Macclesfield.*

It seems probable that under the Saxons, a Church existed in Macclesfield attached to the Court, which was ruined by the reckless hands of the invaders. The present Parochial Chapel, dedicated to St. Michael, dates its foundation from King Edward I. and his Queen Eleanor, in 1278, and was consecrated by the Bishop of St. Asaph. The chapelry comprises the nine townships of Macclesfield, Sutton, Wincle, Wildboarclough, Macclesfield Forest, Kettleshulme, Hurdsfield, Rainow, and Pott Shrigley, and was made dependant by King Edward on the mother Church of Prestbury.

The Parochial Chapel is endowed with £800 private benefaction, and £1200 parliamentary grant. The stipend, (including an annual sum of £50 from the Treasury to the Minister as Queen's Preacher,) amounts to £220, exclusive of the Parsonage House, which was formerly situated

---

*Of the trade of Macclesfield, a slight mention will be found in the appendix, with some notice of other matters of strictly local interest.

on Parsonage Green, and sold by the Corporation in 1780, but on a claim being made by the Minister in 1817, the present house in Beach Lane, built by Mr. Heapy, was assigned to him and his successors.

The present fabric consists of a tower, nave, with side aisles and galleries, a chancel, and two private Chapels on the south side. The early history of this now handsome fabric is uncertain. The tower, which is of the perpendicular style, we should suppose to have been erected as early as 1540, and an arch on the right of the organ gallery belongs probably to the same period.

It was formerly surmounted by a "large steeple spire," which is mentioned in 1585, but was demolished by the pious hands of the Puritans about 1640. The Chapel was partly rebuilt in 1740, at a cost of £1000; but we are indebted for its internal improvements to the Rev. Laurence Heapy, during whose ministry, in 1819–20 the chancel and east end were rebuilt, a small gallery called the old loft which obstructed the view removed, and the present noble and spacious chancel erected, containing a most exquisitely painted window, representing our Saviour, Moses, and the Four Evangelists. The stained glass in the smaller windows, previously in the Guildhall, was liberally presented by the Corporation, who had before contributed the handsome donation of £100 towards the chancel window. The organ, built in 1804 by the predecessors of Hill, has a very fine tone, and the choir is very effective. The coup d'eil from the west entrance is very imposing, and the dim aisles seen "in the soft glimmerings of a sleepy light," may well bespeak the beauty of holiness; to view this noble pile, crowded (as on a late occasion,) with the proud and the humble all prostrate in prayer, must cast, before the eye of the devout, a veil of ecstacy.

The Savage Chapel on the south side of the Church, is our next object of interest, but as our limits will not permit us to describe at length the splendid monuments of pride, and trace the records of each mouldering stone, we must reluctantly glance only for a moment at this small but honoured pile. The entrance is enriched with fine armorial shields, and over a projecting window are the arms of England and of the Savages.

The east window, formerly of stained glass, has been blocked up, and in the interior are corbals and canopied niches, now falling to decay, as we grieve to say are also monuments of a later date. On the north side next the Church, are two altar tombs with alabaster figures of warriors of the Savage family, but with no date or inscription to preserve their memory. Opposite these, remain two altar tombs similarly ornamented, but with the figures removed, and on the same side, another exquisitely finished, with alabaster figures of Sir John Savage, the seventh knight of that name, and Elizabeth his wife, 1528. Handsome mural monuments under stately canopies, perpetuate the names of the eighth Sir John Savage and Elizabeth his wife, 1597, and that of Thomas

Earl Rivers, deceased 1694, whose effigies is sculptured in white marble by Staunton, with a fulsome description of his titles and family; Lady Colchester, probably his daughter-in-law, was buried here 1686. Here is also a gravestone, much worn but still bearing the figure of a churchman with hands raised in prayer, said to be that of George Savage, father of the cruel Bishop Bonner, who died 1552; and a curious tablet is fixed on the wall to Roger Legh of Ridge, 1506, with a Latin inscription, and figures of Roger, his children, and the Pope, who is supposed to utter these words: "The p'don for saying of v pater nost; v aves, and a cred is xxvi thousand yeres and xxvi dayes of pardon." The Chapel now belongs to Earl Cholmondeley.

In the chancel is an altar tomb with recumbent figures, representing Sir John and Katherine Savage, 1495, parents of the Archbishop, and opposite this a recumbent figure of a knight, but without any clue to the name. Of the Savages also repose here Sir John, ninth of the name, 1615, Sir Thomas his son and Mary his wife, 1635, and the first Earl Rivers, 1654, about which time this Chapel was greatly repaired. The founder of this Chapel was Archbishop Savage in 1500, whose heart is supposed to have been buried near the entrance, and who, tradition adds, projected a College of Canons here.

The Legh Chapel, lying on the south side, and repaired in a plain style, contains a marble monument to Letticia Legh, of Lyme, 1648, and to Thomas, her son, 1697, together with a brass plate containing a quaint inscription, and the following rude but striking memorial.

> Here lyethe the bodie of Perkin a Legh
> That for King Richard the death did die
> Betrayed for righteousness
> And the bones of Sir Peers his sonne
> That with King Henrie the fift did wonne
> In Paris.

In the Church are tablets to Wm. Legh, 1630, Caleb Pott, 1690, Thos. Brancker, 1696, Joseph Downes (of the Shrigley family) 1731, all masters of the Free Grammar School; and under an inscription to John Brownswerd, 1589, are the following lines by Thomas Newton, his pupil.

> Alpha poetarum Coryphœus grammaticorum
> Flos pœdagogorum hac sepelitur humo.

A curious inventory of church articles, taken about 1590, mentions amongst other things, one pair of organs, four bells and a passing bell. Under the tablet to William Legh, is a curious figure of a churchman cut in two blocks of stone. Previous to the alteration of the Church, it was hidden by the pews; this might probably be the Protodidasculus, (as he termed himself.)

In the Legh Chapel, lies uncared for, a handsome but mutilated font, in our opinion bearing the stamp of the fifteenth century. We believe that it was lately rescued by a gentleman well known for his antiquarian researches, from the pollutions of a farm yard. It possibly might have been the original font, the present one having been presented by Mr. Hooley in 1740.

We would remark *en passant* on the melancholy desolation in which the Legh and Savage Chapels are suffered to lie. The monuments are fast falling to decay, and the proud nobles who lie here already mourn the loss of some mutilated limbs.

St. Michael's Chapel, usually called *par excellence* the Old Church, has for twelve years enjoyed the talents of the Rev. W. C. Cruttenden, as its Minister. The Rev. J. Bradley is the present Curate.

Christ Church, a large edifice of brick, with a rather unsightly tower, was erected in 1775 by Charles Roe, Esq. to whom there is a handsome monument by Bacon, in the chancel. The interior is very imposing, containing spacious galleries with sittings altogether for more than 1800. The patronage is vested in C. S. Roe, Esq. the descendant of the founder, and it has an endowment of £100 per annum.

A large congregation attend on the ministry of the Rev. W. Pollock, and the Rev. J. Brewster, is the present Curate. A Sunday School directly attached to the Church is contemplated.

The Free Grammar School was originally founded by Sir John Percival " born fast by Maxfield, and late Maire of London," in 1502, together with a chantry suppressed at the Dissolution, for the " maintenance of a preest and scolemaistre who may be a man graduate, to the better relievying with spirituale comforte of all the contre there, as by prechyng and techyng and good example givyng." The original Trustees named by him are Edward Fytton, Rauf Damport, John Sutton the elder of the Rygge, and Roger his eldest son, John Bridge of Edgley, Reignold Oldfield, and John his son, John Worth of Tetrynton and John his son, Thomas Sherygley of Berystowe and Thos. his son, Roger Rowe and Richard his son. A new foundation took place under King Edward VI. in 1552, and in 1774 an act was passed to confirm the sales and purchases of the Governors, and to improve the benefits of the foundation. The revenues are vested in fourteen trustees elected according to the original charter, but obliged to be resident in the Parish. The old School House and grounds, situate near to the Old Church, were sold in 1750 to Nathaniel Bradock and John Stafford, and the existing buildings were then erected on the present site purchased from Sir R. Davenport at the west end of the town in King Edward Street (originally Back Street.)

The Free Grammar School in its earlier days could boast of many elegant and first rate scholars, as names given elsewhere in this sketch will testify. Among its later masters may be mentioned the Rev. Dr. Ingles, afterwards Head Master of Rugby, Rev. Dr. Davies, and Rev. Dr. Newbold.—Rev. W. A. Osborne, of Trin. Coll. Cambridge, is the present Head Master, and Rev. J. B. Bennett, Second Master.

In 1745 the Pretender held his Court for two days at the Grammar School, then belonging to Sir Peter Davenport, a staunch Whig, and the Duke of Cumberland slept soon after at Mr. Stafford's in Jordangate, (a house now subject it is said to ghostly invaders.) This gentleman was notorious for his high Tory principles.

ANTIQUITIES.

Many may feel inclined to smile at the very mention of the antiquities of a town so totally indebted to modern improvements for its present eminence, but yet it contains a ruin perhaps little known, but certainly worthy of the serious reflection of every antiquarian. We allude to the building supposed to have been once the castle of Humphrey the great Duke of Buckingham, who was slain in 1459 at the battle of Northampton. The supposition we believe rests on the authority of Wm. Smith 1585, and Webb 1582, the former of whom calls it "a huge place all of stone now gone to decay," but we find not the slightest historical connection between the town and the Dukes of Buckingham, except the slight notice under Bosley.

This castellated mansion or old manor house, as Webb terms it, where tradition reports the Duke to have lived in princely style, now exists only in an ancient porch, the ceiling of which with the ornamental bosses is very perfect, as also a rude figure on the exterior, in the premises of Mr. Wood, ironmonger. Part of the old wall is also remaining, with a pointed arch of considerable antiquity, and an artificial terrace in the adjacent premises of Mr. Sargent, postmaster, seems to have been the castle yard of this mysterious mansion.

The three principal gates of the fortified town of Macclesfield are still preserved in the names of Jordan, and Wall, and Chester Gates. The former derived its title from Jordan de Macclesfield, living 1347, one of a family of Stayley, who held considerable property in this chapelry. And the proper name of the river in this part, is by some considered to be the Jordan, but we find no mention of it under this title. The question is not very easy of solution, unless we suppose the stream flowing through Macclesfield and Sutton to be called the Jordan, till its junction with the Shrigley brook, which perhaps was originally the Bollin, giving name to Bollington, and afterwards styled the Dean, but certainly so called before 1470, as the name of Dean Row then occurs. Wall-Gate seems to be a corruption and the name derived from the Town Well.

Macclesfield Park, lying at the south west of the town, near the Congleton road, and still retained in the names of Park House, and the road extending from Parsonage Green to the Congleton road, called Park Lane, after the Earldom lapsed to the Crown, was held by the Savages and their successors the Cholmondeleys, from whom it was purchased by John Ryle, Esq., of Henbury, and sold on building leases.

Castle Field, on the right of Park Lane, and now occupied by the factory buildings of Messrs. Wardle, is said to have been the site of the palace of the Earls, or as some would prefer, that of the mansion of the Savages, and to have been the birth place of the Archbishop, but this opinion is unsupported by authority.

Walley Heys, a field belonging to the School Trust, is supposed, from the inequalities of surface and from its name, to have contained some ancient buildings, and this is somewhat confirmed by the land adjoining being called the Town Field.

Gallows Field, where executions formerly took place under the tribunals of the Earl's Justiciary, extended from the site of the Romish Chapel to Mr. Pearson's present factory in Chester Road.

Bate Hall in Chestergate, now a public house, but with its rude buildings still ranged round a small court in the old style, was the residence of the Stopfords of Saltersford, ancestors of the Earl of Courtown, who also holds lands adjoining those of the School near the Bollin.

Worth Hall, also seated in Chestergate on a site now lying waste owing to an unfortunate litigation, was the occasional residence of Archbishop Savage.

Stapelton Hall, the residence of the family of that name in Upton, but now completely ruined, Ogden Hall, which belonged to the Swettenhams, and Pickford Hall on Park Green, once the seat of the Pickfords, a family who arrived at civic distinction in Macclesfield about 1600, and on the site of which is the present residence of Mr. Lallemand, exist only in name.

In the Back Wallgate is an old building roofed with stone called the Town Well, in appearance a building of great antiquity. The well has been walled up and a pump was erected in 1834.

The King's Bakehouse retained by the Crown till 1818, and now belonging to Mr. Corbishley and used as a warehouse, is the " furnus villœ" mentioned in the original charter, which obliged the burgesses to grind at the Earl's mill and to bake at his oven.

The Corporation as at present constituted consists of 48 Councillors, out of which 12 Aldermen are elected. The representatives in Parliament for this, the Northern Division of the County, are W. T. Egerton, Esq., and the Hon. E. J. Stanley.

The Members for the Borough are J. Brocklehurst and T. Grimsditch, Esqrs. The present Recorder, elected in 1833, is W. C. Townshend, Esq. acting without salary; and the Mayor, a gentleman of the highest respectability, is T. Wardle, Esq.

Of the public buildings and institutions of Macclesfield, as we do not assume the duties of a guide, we shall speak briefly. In Duke Street, a spacious edifice was erected in 1813 by voluntary contributions, for the purposes of a Church National School. It consists of two good rooms; the upper one containing an excellent organ. The children now instructed amount in the Day School to 283, in the Sunday School to 385. The scholars regularly attend the services of the Established Church, and the School is supported by annual subscriptions, amounting in 1839 to about £70.

A large Sunday School in Roe Street, a building of considerable size but little elegance, was erected in the same year, at a cost of £5639.

On Park Green is a public library, established in 1770, which is well furnished with works of modern literature, and contains a valuable collection of public records presented by the Commissioners. Adjoining this building is an excellent News Room. In 1814 a Dispensary in Mill Street was first established, and has since been supported by annual subscriptions reaching in the last year £405. An estimate of its usefulness may be formed from the fact of 1585 persons having been relieved in 1839.

An English School from the design of Mr. Hayley is in the course of erection near Christ Church, under the sanction of the Governors of the Free Grammar School, and the building, which is of stone, when finished, will be a considerable ornament. The institution will, we believe, resemble those already formed at Birmingham and other places.

The Guildhall erected in 1825 at an estimate of £4579, contains, besides Justice Rooms, Offices, &c., a handsome Assembly Room with Music Gallery, for size and elegance second to none in the county, but unfortunately seldom used for its original purposes. There is also a spacious Butter Market attached to it, and the Town Gaol adjoining was rebuilt at the same time.

A handsome building on Park Green, next to the Library, is the Banking House of Messrs. Daintry, Ryle, and Co., and the Messrs. Brocklehursts have a similar establishment in King Edward Street.

A new and elegant structure is contemplated for the Savings Bank at present occupying the house next to Mr. Ryle's Bank.

A Public Cemetery is also on the tapis ; and here we must record a passing tribute to the zeal and energy of the citizens of Macclesfield in promoting every laudable and useful work, two additional Churches at Broken Cross and on the Common being already named.

A Theatre of wood formerly existed in Chestergate, at which Miss Mellon, late Duchess of St. Alban's, is said to have made her début, and a noble instance of her generosity is recorded in a pension to a fellow actor of the name of Dyer. The present edifice in Mill Street was opened in 1811, but the drama here, as elsewhere in the provinces, is altogether on the decline. The front part of the building is devoted to the purposes of an Operative Conservative News Room.

The ancient part of the town lies behind the Market-place around the Shambles, but there are here no houses of interest. In King Edward Street, a stately old mansion adjoining the Police Office appears to have been once a place of consequence. It was inhabited by Mr.

F

Stone, and belongs to the Unitarian Chapel, formerly Presbyterian. In Chestergate are several venerable piles of olden days, and a curious half timbered house, now a small inn, the most ancient building in the town. The town is tolerably paved and well lighted with gas, first introduced in 1815.

The Macclesfield Canal, first projected about 1796, was commenced in 1826, under the guidance of Mr. Telford, and was opened for the purposes of trade in 1831. From the Peak Forest Canal in Marple it passes through nine townships of this parish, and joins the Trent and Mersey Canal at Church Lawton.

Among several pretty residences in Macclesfield we must especially notice Park House, late the seat of John Ryle, Esq. and now in the occupation of Mr. Procter and Mr. Stringer; and Westbrook, adjoining Upton township, a most beautiful spot now uninhabited, but the property of Charles Wood, Esq. Park Brook, on the Chester road, is the pleasing abode of T. Grimsditch, Esq.; and a handsome house on the same road, called Summer Hill, is the residence of C. S. Roe, Esq.

In Macclesfield are large and handsome Dissenting Places of Worship belonging to the Wesleyans, Independents, and other sects; and on Chester Road a handsome Romish Chapel (opposite the former building) is approaching completion, for architectural elegance doing great credit to the design of Mr. Pugin.

It is not our intention to enter into detail of the constitution of the Courts of the Forest of Macclesfield, as now that its privileges have fallen into disuse the discussion would appear tedious. The office of Master Forester and Hereditary Steward, now merely honorary, has been vested in the Stanleys for more than 400 years. The deputy Stewardship is held by James Leigh, Esq., of Belmont, and Mr. W. Brocklehurst is Clerk of the Courts. Two Courts are held half yearly for trial of civil causes.

The Grand Serjeancy of Macclesfield Hundred has been held by the Davenports for nearly 600 years, and formerly granted the power of life and death over the inhabitants of the Hundred. To the Serjeant fell all the forfeited property, and sixpence for the proclamation of every fair, which he was obliged to make in person. The Davenports adopted their crest, a felon's head coupeé, from this office.

We must be allowed to glance for a moment at some loyal and brave families to whom, though silent in the "narrow house" with perhaps their name forgotten, some slight memorial is due. The Blagges of Chestergate, the Shrigleys and Davenports of Sutton, the Mottersheads and the Deanes, the Pickfords and the Birtles, the Lunts, the Worthingtons and the Staffords filled civic offices in the 17th century, with many others, as the Claytons and the Hulleys, still retaining their respectable position in society.

SUTTON OR SUTTON DOWNES.

Sutton Downes an extensive township, 4½ miles in diameter, containing about 7808 imhabitants, and comprising 3181 acres and 1456 houses, lies within the chapelry of Macclesfield, and occupies a large portion of the wild but now cultivated hills of the forest.

Sutton Hall beautifully seated in well wooded grounds at the junction of two brawling mountain brooks, was the residence of a family who had the estates granted to them by Hugh Kevelioc 6th Earl, about 1170, on the right of forest service. From this time the family continued in direct male succession for twelve generations till about 1500, when John grandson of Sir William Sutton of Burton Lazars in Leicestershire, and nephew of Sir Richard Sutton, founder of Brazennoze College, Oxford, of the same branch, inherited the property. After five generations the estates passed by death of Richard, slain in a tumult in Chester 1601, to Sir Humphrey Davenport of Bramhall, whose granddaughter brought it into the Fauconburg family, and it is now the property of the Earl of Lucan, the existing part of the mansion being occupied by the Misses Bent. A wing only of the original building remains, and this with its old hall and ancient relics, as some carved wooden figures, is all that now remains of this noble pile. Sir Richard Sutton of the branch of this family at Burton Lazars, founded Brazenose College 1514, and was the author of the Orcharde of Sion and other works. The late Countess of Lucan for some time made the hall her residence.

The Hollins, a small farm house with a modern cottage residence attached, on an eminence above the canal, gave name to a family about 1220, a branch of whom settled on an estate at Cophurst Edge, and the ninth of this family was Ralph Hollinshed, the Chronicler, who also inherited the Hollins estate, and in whom the male line terminated. The prospect from the eminence above the house is enchanting, including Mowcop and the Staffordshire hills, and extending far beyond Congleton. The Hollins, the name of which is also preserved in Hollin Lane, became about 1659, the property of Joseph Stonehewer of Foden Bank, and is now vested in his descendants.

The Cophurst estate after being temporarily possessed by the Leghs of Lyme, passed to Mr. Bullock, and since then has been sold in lots. The Traffords were a family residing here about 1600. Hoghlegh was an estate held by forest service and gave name to a family before 1340, but passed to the Leghs of Lyme about 1560.

The Downes Manor, held by free forestry with Taxal, became at an early period merged with the estates of Sutton Hall and Ridge. Ridge, the residence of the Leghs, a branch of the Lyme family, from 1431 to 1731, and acquired by marriage with the Alcocks, is now a humble cottage situated above the new Church at Sutton, and a little below the road leading to Cophurst. The sole vestiges of this ancient seat are the moat lately planted, and a stone placed in the present building bearing date 1584. The Estate passed by purchase to William Norton, M.D. of Buxton, and thence to his great nephew W. Smyth, Esq. Professor of Modern History in Cambridge, Author of English Lyrics, and other Works. The house is tenanted by a worthy old couple by name Hall, who seem to take great interest in their lowly ruin.

A little nearer Sutton is an old house, but newly fronted, bearing date 1693, with the name of its occupant Henry Cherry, the representative of a family who held much property in Macclesfield, and were for centuries the agents of the Savages here. We meet with their name in 1600.

Langley Hall, a stately building of stone, and prettily seated on the banks of a clear rivulet, with the hills in the background, but now obtruded on by the adjacent factories of Mr. Smith, was from 1651 to 1808 the residence of a family originally of the adjoining township of Wincle. It is now the property of Mr. Yates, but as the informant expressed herself " the family are all scattered." The house is ancient but in miserable repair.

The Oaks, now a small half-timbered farm house on an eminence near the junction of the old and new Leek roads, was the residence of Philip Arderne son of the Aldford family before 1640, and his son James was living there 1694. The estate afterwards was vested in the Meres, and in 1820 in Dr. Davies of Macclesfield.

Foden Bank, so named from a family in the township as early as 1600, is the residence of the Rev. J. Burnet. The Byrons, now occupied as a school, formerly belonged to a family of that name before 1530, who were by marriage connected with the Stanleys of Alderley. Mr. C. Wood has lately built here a handsome mansion in the Elizabethan style, termed the Elms; and Mr. Parrott the respected Town Clerk, resides at a pretty place in this Township, about two miles from Macclesfield, called Green Bank. The Macclesfield Canal flows through the Sutton Hall estate, and near it is an old house, now falling to decay and by tradition reported to be haunted.

A loyal cavalier of the name of Creswell, in Sutton, is denounced by Bradshaw as keeping a horse called Stoned Robin, which " he meaneth to be the death of the Protector. He liveth like an outlaw, and cannot be captured."

The Church of St. George, in Sutton, erected in 1822, by shares, at a cost of £4400, was for six years the scene of the ministry of Mr. McAll, before Chaplain of the Sunday School. In 1828 it was licensed by the present Bishop, (the first act of his episcopal functions,) for the services of the establishment, and the Rev. W. Wales was appointed Minister, succeeded by the Rev. John Burnet in 1832. In July, 1834, St. George's Church was consecrated, together with a burial ground, probably of the value of £600, presented by Mr. Ryle. It contains 1600 sittings, and is endowed with £1000.

In 1835, an Infant School was established by means of a grant from the Treasury of £400, and the proceeds of a Bazaar amounting to £1150. One hundred and fifty children are here educated, and in the Sunday School opened in 1837, 400 receive every sabbath a sound religious education.

The Church of St. James now in the course of erection, is situated on an eminence above Sutton Hall, and is built for the spiritual welfare of an important district situated beyond the toll bar on the Leek road, comprising 247 houses and 1200 inhabitants. The style is plain, but in good taste from the design of Mr. Hayley.

The Church will contain 330 sittings. The site has been presented by the Rev. Dr. Newbold.

HURDSFIELD.

A large but uninteresting township included in the Chapelry and Borough of Macclesfield, in 1831 nursed a population of 3083 which had increased three-fold in ten years, and now probably reaches 5000. To a considerable portion of these inhabitants the silk factories afford employment. The Church dedicated to the Holy Trinity is a handsome Gothic building built from the design of Mr. Hayley of Manchester, and affords accommodation for more than 870. The site was given by Professor Smyth, and the Church consecrated by the Bishop of Chester in October, 1839. A Sunday School has been already formed, where 230 children are educated, and a building will be erected for the purpose in a short time.

Swanscoe Park in this township prettily situated on the Rainow side, and still retaining part of its old wall, was held of old by the Earls of Derby as stewards of the forest, and is traditionally reported to have been one of the places where the Duke of Buckingham so mysteriously associated with Macclesfield, kept up such princely state. It is now vested by purchase in Mr. Ward.

KETTLESHULME.

Kettleshulme, a township situate among the dreary wilds of the forest hills, on the left of the road to Chapel-en-le-Frith, in 1831 had a decreasing population of 232. The tenure of the land is copyhold, and the grounds command a fine prospect of the vale and Church of Taxal and the high lands at the confines of the Lyme estate.

WILDBOARCLOUGH.

Wildboarclough is a district offering considerable interest in connexion with the wild and merry outlaws, for whose capture the Davenports received two shillings and a salmon, but now that the days are fled when

Mery it was in the grene forest,
Among the leves grene.
Where men hunt east and west,
Wyth bowes and arrowes keen.

The only object of importance is the natural tumulus called Shutlingslow, a rock rising from a very elevated valley, and presenting itself in a sugar-loaf form to the eye in every view of the district. Below this hill on the Derbyshire side is a solitary factory. Wildboarclough, which lies above Cophurst Edge, 6½ miles from Macclesfield, and adjacent to the Buxton and Congleton road, contained in 1831, a rude and uncultivated population of 476, and there is we believe a dissenting place of worship. A remarkable instance of the salubrity of the neighbourhood occurs in this township, two deaths only (and those of persons whose united ages amounted to 175) having taken place within the last six months.

WINCLE.

Wincle, situated on the right of the Congleton and Buxton road, six miles from Macclesfield, and on the edge of the County, Dane Bridge in Staffordshire being adjoining, contained a grange of the monks of Combermere, now vested in Mr. Daintry. Beneath a hill planted with firs, which commands a wild view of the adjacent moors, including Swithamley Park, the property of William Brocklehurst, Esq., lies the Chapel erected in 1642, and since rebuilt with stone, and again about 1820, repaired and new pewed. The interior is very plain, containing only two simple monumental slabs. In 1717 there was no pulpit or communion table, and there had been no preaching for half a year past. The Chapel is endowed with £400 private benefaction, £600 Royal bounty, and £1,300 grant from Parliament, and is in the gift of the Vicar of Prestbury. The Rev. J. Bostock is the present Minister. The curacy is valued at £116, and there are sittings for 260 persons.

RAINOW.

Rainow, a long straggling village situate 2½ miles from Macclesfield, adjoining Hurdsfield, contains a population of about 2400, chiefly employed in the silk manufacture. The Chapel, still unconsecrated, but rebuilt about 1700, is a plain building containing accommodation for 260 persons. A school formerly attached to it, is we believe now in the hands of the Wesleyans, and supported by voluntary donations. The curacy, endowed with £200 private benefaction, £800 Royal bounty, and £1,800 grant, is in the gift of the Vicar of Prestbury, and now held by the Rev. W. Parke. The annual income is £100. Rainow seems to have been the place of junction for the Roman roads from Condate and Manchester to Buxton. Urns of that period have been found, and a station probably existed here, an opinion confirmed by the name of Kerridge.

Saltersford in this township, lying in a wild valley approached by a steep lane leading from the Chapel-en-le-Frith road, by the Blue Boar Inn, gives the second title to the Earls of Courtown, the second Earl having been created Baron of Saltersford in 1794. James Stopford of this place served in the Parliament's army 1641, and acquired large estates in Meath, Ireland. The present Earl of Courtown is the sixth in descent from him, and succeeded in 1835. Some of the family resided in the neighbourhood for many years after the civil wars. The hall, beautifully seated in a peaceful dingle hard by a gentle stream, is said to have been built in 1594, and still bears the date 1653 over the remains of the doorway. It is now a small farm house. On an eminence near it is Jenkin Chapel, so called from Jenkin Cross of which there are slight remains, dedicated to St. John. It was erected at John Slack's expense in 1733, and is endowed with £200 private benefaction, and £800 Royal bounty, the yearly value being £47. The building, which is of grey stone, is rude, but has a turretted belfry, and the chapel was consecrated about 1793 ; the Rev. E. Luscombe is the present Minister. The population amounts to 103. Jenkin Chapel contains 100 sittings, and attached to it is a Sunday and Day School, educating about thirty children.

In the township of Rainow beside the Buxton road, is the residence of Mr. Hulley, "The One House," seated among the hills, but presenting a rich and luxuriant scene of hill and dale. The Hulleys, probably a branch of the Hoghleghs, sometime proud Forresters of Sutton, were settled here before 1650.

The small township of Macclesfield Forest, seated in the very heart of the wilds, and apart from the busy haunts of man, is tenanted by a homely population of 220. The situation is deliciously retired, the sole approach being by a rough track from Stoneway Turnpike on the Buxton road. The hamlet consists of the Chapel, School House, *Inn*, and a few grey cottages. The old Chapel erected, as it is believed, at three different periods (a stone bearing the date of 1673) was removed in 1834 to give place to a neat edifice of brick containing nearly 200 sittings. The expense was defrayed by a donation of £100 from the Earl of Derby and £30 private contributions. There is a Sunday and Day School here, the former educating 40 and the latter 20 children. The master, by the kind liberality of the Rev. G. Mounsey the present minister appointed in 1798, has a house and garden rent free, and a small salary. The patronage is vested in the Earl of Derby. The village schoolmaster here strongly reminds us of Wilkie's picture, and is a fine specimen of a class now almost extinct.

POToT SHRIGLEY.

" And then the family
extinguished in him, and the good old name
only to be remembered on a tombstone !
A name that has gone down from sire to son
so many generations."

The foregoing lines seem peculiarly applicable to a family who for so many centuries adorned this fair estate, but now have set, like stars that have shone, and we only hear the sound of their praise. Although the rich demesne has fallen into the hands of a gentleman whose name for liberality and good deeds is already graven on the hearts of his poorer neighbours, there still must lurk in the mind a sympathy with the past, and memory will carry us back to feudal dignities now almost extinct. To trace the fortunes of the noble line of the Downes, to speak of their alliance with the Egertons, Leghs, Davenports, and many a fair dame of high estate, would carry us too far. We must content ourselves with a slight survey. Robert de Downes may claim to be the founder of the family. He assumed his name from Downes in Sutton, and his descendants were Foresters for many years. He seems to have acquired this estate by marriage with the heiress of the Shrigley family about 1270. The fourth from him added to the honours of the house about 1400 by alliance with Agnes de Hulme, who brought him the Manor of Worth and the Ratones lands in Upton, held by forest service. During 550 years, and through twenty generations, the Manor was handed down from father to son, till in 1815 the estates were purchased from Edward Downes, Esq. the last of the ancient race, (who died in 1819) by William Turner, Esq. of Mill Hill, M.P. for Blackburn, in whom the property is now vested. The sole surviving representative of " the old family " is the lady of Mr. Panter, Northend, Fulham, her only sister having gone to her fathers at Shrigley in 1839.

The Hall is an elegant modern Mansion erected in 1819, and looks out upon a park enriched with stately trees and open green. The ground extends as far as Lyme Park, and on a beautiful eminence is a *modern ruin* erected by Mr. Downes.

The Chapel next must call for our attention. It was founded by Geoffrey Downes in 1492, for " the maintaining a priest who shall continually and dayley bee dwelling and be at comyns table and board within Pott Shrigley and who shall keep noe horse ne hawke ne hound." The old embattled tower still remains, and the appearance of the interior from the west door is very striking, and exhibits a very good instance of modern taste, having been fitted up in a collegiate style by Mr. Downes. The altar is very much elevated, and in the chancel are slabs to the memory of Edward and Peter Downes. In the east window remain some rich but faded relics of stained glass. The design appears to be that of a female kneeling, and under the arms of the founder is the following inscription now scarcely legible,

Orate pro bone valence Galfridi Downes
Qui istam capellam fieri fecit.

The entrance door is enriched with panels of modern stained glass, and the roof being of painted oak gives the chapel a venerable appearance. A neat organ gallery stands at the West end, and the seats designed for the choir are now occupied by the Sunday School. The side aisles are separated from the nave by pointed arches. The view from the Church porch is very interesting. Before you the frail memorials of the dead, with many a holy text or simple rhyme; beyond is nature's carpet stretched afar with solemn hanging woods, well suited to the quiet beauty of the place, closing this rural scene. Beside the churchyard is the village school, a neat building of Mr. Turner's erection in 1832. Outside the chancel stands a time-worn cross, in appearance a relic of the 16th century, but having nothing sufficiently striking to stamp its date. The chapel is endowed with £3000, including an annual grant of £3 from the Treasury, it would seem in lieu of lands retained by the Crown at the dissolution. The annual stipend is £120, and the Rev. J. Sumner is the highly esteemed Minister, under whose especial guidance the school is conducted, and educates 150 children. John Barlow, 1684, bequeathed £5 annually, for the support of a master. The patronage of the chapel is vested in Mr. Turner, and previous to the erection of the fabric at Bollington, it was as it were the Mother Church of the neighbouring townships.

Pott Hall, a fair old mansion near the Church, was for centuries the seat of a family bearing the local name, now represented by Henry Potts, Clerk of the Peace of the County, whose ancestor about 50 years ago disposed of a tract of land called Cockshut Hey, formerly attached to it. It is now the residence of the highly intelligent and opulent manufacturer Martin Swindells, Esq.

Beristall Hall, now a decayed farm house, but in the most lovely situation that the neighbourhood can boast of, overlooking the sweet vale of Shrigley, with Alderley edge terminating the distant prospect, was long the seat of a branch of the Shrigleys, and sold by them (afterwards resident in Sutton) to Alderman Lunt of Macclesfield, from whom it passed to Legh Watson, Esq., ancestor of our highly esteemed townswoman Miss Watson, of Chestergate. It was annexed to the Shrigley estates by E. Downes, together with Ridacre Hall (now ruined) also the property of Mr. Watson. There are also tracts of lands within the township bearing the permanent names of Potts Moor, Bakestone Dale, the Blake Hey, and the Holmes. From the vicinity of Bakestone Dale the Church and village are seen to great perfection. The original name of the township is a point at which we break a lance with the local antiquarians. Instead of being Pott within Shrigley (as by some plausibly

G

contended) we are inclined to believe that it originally bore the peculiar title of Pott, and received its second name from a family settled here as early as the 12th century. The population of Shrigley amounts to about 334. Several collieries are worked in the township.

LOCAL CUSTOMS AND SUPERSTITIONS.

———

> " Thy wakes, thy quintels, here thou hast,
> Thy May-poles too with garlands graced,
> Thy morrice dance, thy Whitsun ale,
> Thy shearing feast, which never fail."
>
> HERRICK.

The true spirit of the English character is nowhere more beautifully illustrated than in the village festival, the grey headed sires seated beneath the yew tree's shade, the sprightly damsels glowing with nature's exercise, the sturdy ploughman proud in his Sunday suit. But this, we fear, is now an ideal scene of olden days.

The remark of Drayton that the Cheshire men of all England most to ancient customs cleave, is still verified, though the May-pole is here as elsewhere in a measure superseded by the scientific Lecture Room, and the games of Merry England in the olden time have been sagely discovered to be unsuited to the intellectual spirit of the age. Even Cheshire, though her yeomen still maintain the boast of retaining their primitive character, has suffered from this tide of innovation, and in our own neighbourhood the Queen of May has abdicated her flowery throne, and the village green is no longer enlivened by the merry dance.

The wake, commemorative of the Patron Saint to whom the Church is dedicated and so called from vigil or waking, still retains its primitive character. On this occasion all the relations meet round the social hearth and attend Divine Service, and though the custom may undoubtedly lead to riot and excess, it would be better to improve its character than to extirpate a feeling so blended with affection to our ancient Church. On Easter Sunday it is the custom at Prestbury for the villagers to assemble and drink spiced ale, and we are assured, that no excess ever occurs there.

Mock plays were not long ago performed in private houses; and the customs of souling or begging soul cakes, on All Souls eve, is still practised. The song concluded with the following simple remonstrance:

> I hope you will prove kind with your apples and strong beer,
> We'll come no more a souling until another year.

The customs of begging corn at Christmas and eggs at Easter, being not peculiar to Cheshire, we shall omit, and the practice of lifting " more honoured in the breach than the observance," is also prevalent in the neighbouring counties.

The Maypole is no more ; but it is still the custom on the first of May, for lovers to place birchen boughs over the doors of their lovers, and an alder branch is consecrated to the dwelling of a scold.

At Appleton a ceremony took place of old, called the Bawming of Appleton Thorn, and consisted in adorning an old hawthorn tree in the middle of the town.

The customs of strewing rushes in the Church, and hanging up long poles with garlands and festoons of flowers, is utterly extinct; but retained at Grasmere and Ambleside, in Westmoreland.

At Knutsford, on festive occasions, white sand is, we believe, now strewed before the door, on which devices are executed, and sometimes flowers scattered around.

A custom peculiar to this county, exists in the neighbourhood of Alderley and elsewhere, among the marlers. A Lord of the Pit is chosen, who receives donations, and then they join hands, making four bows towards the centre, and shouting " Largo." After this they dress up a pole with ribbands and call it " carrying the garland."

The manly game of Cricket is still kept up with much spirit, and at Macclesfield and Knutsford excellent clubs are established.

Quoits is also a favourite pastime on the village green.

The Cucking-stool or Tumbrell existed from time immemorial as a punishment for brawlers, and the Duckin-stool, a similar though distinct instrument, was retained at Macclesfield not many years ago. There is still seen there an iron brank for scolds, called " a brydle for a cruste queane," in old documents.

The tenure of the Taxall Manor held by the Downes' was three blasts of a Bugle-horn at Windgather Rocks and a pepper corn yearly. The Lyke Wake is disused, but the friends of the deceased always assemble in large numbers at Church the Sunday after the funeral, and generally finish the evening in riotous excess.

LEGENDS AND TRADITIONS.

A tradition exists that the celebrated John Bradshaw, of Marple Hall, who presided in the High Court of Justice on the trial of Charles the First, resided for some time at Macclesfield, and that there, on a stone in the churchyard, he wrote the following lines :—

My brother Henry must heir the land,
My brother Frank must be at his command,
Whilst I poor Jack will do that
That all the world will wonder at.

The fabled origin of the Derby cognisance, the Eagle and Child, is well known. The Lord of Latham, 1301—1367, being childless, having by chance or *otherwise*, discovered a beautiful infant in an eagle's eyrie in the park, adopted the boy as his heir, and Isabella the daughter of this child, afterwards Sir Oskeytel Latham, married about 1400 Sir John Stanley, famed for having slain a French warrior in the presence of the King ; whence the Stanleys adopted this crest, retained also by the Lathams of Bradwall, and other branches of this noble family. This legend is variously stated, but is assumed to be founded upon fact, in the History of the Isle of Man, by William Sacheverell, 1702.

The following Legend occurs in a Deed of Augmentation in 1560, which we shall give in the quaint style of the original document :—

"Thomas Venables of Goulborne lynyally dyscendid frome S'r Gilbart Venables coosyn garman to Kynge, William Conqueror, when a terrible Dragon made his abode in the Lordeshippe of Moston, shott hym throwe with an arrowe and afterward with other weapons manfullie slew him, at which instant tyme the said dragon was devowringe of a child."

The account adds, that he obtained the Lordship of Moston from this chivalrous exploit, and the legend still gains credence with the peasantry of Moston, where the story is preserved in a piece of water called Dragon's Pool ; and a dragon (afterwards changed to a wyvern) was the crest of the family.

Although our fair friends may charge us with heresy in classing the lays of Nixon amongst legendary lore, we are rather inclined to believe, that in spite of these archives deposited in the mysterious room at Vale Royal, which is only visited once by the heir of the house, in spite of the wonderful accounts attested by ladies of high degree, in spite of his authentic portrait, that either this old gentleman never existed or lived nearer to our own age than the 15th century. Tradition says that he was born at Bridge End House in Over in 1457, of poor agricultural parents, that amongst other prophecies he foretold that an heir should be born to the Cholmondeley family when an eagle should sit on the top of a house, and that the heir of Oulton should be hanged at his own gate, verified it is said by the death of John Egerton in 1732 by a fall from his horse. Having, on account of the fulfilment of his prophecy respecting the Battle of Bosworth, been sent for to Court, he was there, according to his own saying, starved to death by accident.

BIOGRAPHICAL NOTICES.

Thomas Savage, youngest son of Sir John Savage the fourth Knight of Clifton, and Catharine sister of Thomas Stanley Earl of Derby, was bred a Doctor of Laws in the University of Cambridge, appointed to the See of Rochester in 1492, thence translated to London in 1497, and to the Archbishopric of York in 1501. Tradition names Macclesfield Park and Worth Hall as his reputed birth places, but to which the boast is due seems uncertain. He resided for a time at Mottram Andrew, and gave some lands to the Free Grammar School at Macclesfield. He died at York in 1508, and his body lies buried there, but his heart was deposited in his own chapel at Macclesfield. He was a greater Courtier than Clerk, and very fond of the chace, and, moreover, of a frugal disposition though he rebuilt the Palaces at Scroby and Cawood.

Raphaell Hollinshed, the Chronicler, was born at the Cophurst estate in Sutton, and published his Chronicles in 1577, consisting of different works, and compiled by various hands. His death is supposed to have taken place three years after.

Sir Richard Sutton of Burton Lazars in Leicestershire, but born probably in Prestbury parish, was Governor of the Inner Temple, and Steward of Sion Monastery near Brentford in 1513. He founded Brazennoze, in concert with William Smith, Bishop of Lincoln, whence the following rude couplet—

> Begun by one, but finished by another,
> Sutton, he was my nurse, and Smith my mother.

He is called by an old Chronicler a man of plentiful estate and bountiful hand, and died in 1524.

Sir Humphrey Davenport of Bramhall, married to Mary Sutton of Sutton, studied in the Temple, and was appointed Chief Baron of the Exchequer. He died in 1645, " being a sound Lawyer and upright person."

The connection of the Calveleys of Lea with Mottram, and their alliance with the Leghs of Lyme, require a slight notice of that ancient warrior and valiant knight " Sir Hugh Calveley." To enumerate the noble exploits of this hero of the 14th century is impossible. Of his more striking achievements we would note his being one of the thirty English who encountered as many Bretons at Josselin, the site of which conflict is called Le Champ des Anglois ; and his burning 26 ships at Boulogne. He was Governor of Calais, and afterwards of Guernsey, and tradition adds that he married Eleanor Queen of Arragon. His death took place 1394.

Sir John Percivale, the founder of Macclesfield Free Grammar School, was born somewhere in the neighbourhood, probably of humble origin. From being the carver of the London Corporation he rose to the high offices of Sheriff and Lord Mayor in 1501, when he was knighted by Henry VII, and in the following year endowed the Grammar School with ten pounds.

LOCAL PROVERBS.

"To live like a Freeholder of Macclesfield, who has neither corn nor hay at Michaelmas," explained thus :—To feed voraciously like a half starved mechanic.

"Maxfield measure, heap and thrutch" (thrust.) Heap measure— when the measure is heaped above the top—as full as it will hold.

"Cheshire chief of men."—Evidently having its origin from themselves.

"Better wed over the mixon than over the moor."—Expressive of the little intercourse the Cestrians of old were inclined to have with their neighbours.

"The Mayor of Altrincham and the Mayor of Over. "The one is a thatcher and the other a dauber."—Two decayed towns, the Mayors of which were elected without any distinct charter.

"As fair as Lady Done and as great as the Earl of Derby."—The Dones of Utkinton were a younger-branch of the Venables of Kinderton. The Lady here immortalized, was a daughter of Mr. Wilbraham.

"Every man is not born to be Vicar of Bowden."—A living in Bucklow hundred, valued £24 in the King's books.

"In dock out nettle."—Expressive of inconstancy. The words repeated with the application of the dock-leaf, said to effect a cure for the sting of a nettle.

"To be knotchelled," i. e. disgraced.

"Stockport Chaise."—A horse with two women riding sideways on it.

"To catch a person napping, as Mosse caught his mare."—The mare alluding to his wife, as the following line explains :—

"till daye come catch him as Mosse his grey mare."

"To have made a good note," as of a good milking cow.

"She hath been in London to call a strea a straw, and a waw a wall."—Meaning, she is too proud to use her native dialect.

"He is got into Cherry's boose," i.e. into an unpleasant situation. Cherry's boose, the stall of the red cow.

"To scold like a wych waller," a salt boiler.

The following distich, though generally known, had its origin from Cheshire :—

The Robin and the Wren
Are God's cock and hen,
The Martin and the Swallow
Are God's mate and marrow.

GLOSSARY.

Of a few words peculiar to Cheshire.

The affinity of the Lancashire and Cheshire dialects is very striking, and some connection is also traced between the "patois" of Cheshire and Norfolk, owing perhaps to their little intercourse with other Counties, in former times.

Agate, "one recovered from sickness," also "one that is employed." "He is agate marling." "Agate a new cart," (making one.)

Agg, to provoke, from Danish "Egger," or French "Agacer."

Alegar, i. e. ale aigre.

Awlung, owing to.

Baggin time, the time of the afternoon luncheon.

Bandy Hewit, a turnspit, derived perhaps from scout.

Bawm, to adorn.

Bloten, fond of, as a child of its nurse.

Boke, to poke, to point at.

Boose, a cow's stall.

Bradow, to cover, as a hen her chickens.

Brewes, slices of bread with fat broth poured over them.

Brosier, a bankrupt.

Bruart, to shoot, as newly sown corn.

Bur, the elder tree.

Cadger, to carry.

Cample, to scold.

Cale, turn "it is my cale now."

Carve, to grow sour, to curdle as milk.

Chunner, to grumble.

Cant, strong, lusty.

Clemm'd, starved with hunger. "I am welly clemm'd."

Cranny, pleasant.

Creem, to pour.

Cobbles, round coals.

Cumberlin, a troublesome fellow.

Deavely, lonely, retired.

Demath, a day's mowing for one man.

Doesom, healthy.

Dree, long, tedius. "A dree rain," i. e. a thick small rain.

Drumble, a ravine with trees.

Eaver, a quarter of the heavens.

Ess, ashes.

Edderings, radlings in a hedge. So Tusser:

> "Save edder and stake
> Strong hedge to make."

Fallgate, a gate across a high road.

Farinkly, decently.

Fettle, to mend.

Fitchet Pie, a pie composed of apples, onions, and bacon, served to labourers at harvest-home.

Flasker, to stifle.

Flurch, a great many; as a flurch of strawberries.

Fliggers, young birds beginning to fly.

Gawn, a gallon.

Glaffer, to flatter.

Gliff, a glimpse.

Glop, to stare.

Guttit, shrovetide; a corruption from good tide.

Gwill, to dazzle.

Gawfin, a clown.

Gooding, to collect money for the poor to feast at Christmas.

Hattle, wild.

Hilling, a coverlet.

Hollin, the holly tree.

By hulch and stulch, by hook and crook.

Kibbow, strong.

Kidcrow, a place for a sucking calf.

Lich Gates, the gates of the churchyard only opened for funerals.

Magging, prating.

Oss, to try, to offer.

Pash, brains.

Quank, quiet.

Rise, a twig.

Leech, a spring in a field forming a swamp;

Selt, chance.

Stiddy, steady.

Skeer, to scour.

Skreen, a wooden settle with a back by a kitchen fire.

Springow, nimble.

Thrippa, to beat.

Thruff and thruff, through and through.

Thrunk, crowded.

Tin, to tin the fire, *i. e.* light.

A threeweek, as a fortnight.

Wheady, measuring more than it appears.

Everywhile stitch, now and then.

Wham, near at hand.

White, to requite.

Yaff, to bark.

APPENDIX.

To the reader of the foregoing pages, the question would naturally suggest itself,—Why, in a sketch of a town and neighbourhood so immediately indebted to manufacture for its present eminence, we have purposely omitted all mention of its commercial interests ? To solve this problem, it must be remembered that we have been tasting "the pleasures of memory, not of hope;" that ours have been dreams and imaginings of the past, not realities of the present. In order, however, to atone for the omission, we proceed to offer a concise history of the trade of Macclesfield.

The staple manufacture of Macclesfield was originally that of silk, mohair, and twist buttons, in use as early as 1650, and mills were erected here for winding silk, and making twist for them. This trade gave rise to a race of hawkers called Flashmen* from a Chapel of the name at the extremity of the county, not far from Wincle. These *worthies*, in concert with the Broken Cross gang (a race of juggling sharpers), used to frequent the fairs, using a canting dialect, and after numerous enormities were at last extirpated by the magistrates.—About 1700 an act passed forbidding the wearing of buttons covered as the coat, and in 1778 this act was attempted to be put in force. This branch of trade was partially superseded by the brass buttons of Birmingham, but is now in a thriving state.

As early as 1700 the silk trade was known in Macclesfield; but Charles Roe, Esq., was the first silk throwster, and erected a mill on Park Green in 1756. A cotton manufactory was built in the Waters in 1795, and the manufacture of silk was started in King Edward-street in 1790.

We should consider Macclesfield, owing to the dampness of its situation, to be by no means a healthy spot, and low fever and scrofula are very prevalent among the lower classes. In the Dispensary the mortality averages one out of 30; high testimony has been borne to the cleanliness of the occupation in the silk factories, to the airiness of the apartments, and apparent good health of the children employed; and four eminent medical men of the town have expressed it as their decided opinion, that there are fewer cases of deformity than formerly.

---

* The name is preserved in the Flash at Butley; but we are inclined to doubt this supposed origin of a word so common in the world of "*slang*."

AGRICULTURAL NOTICE.

The land in the Parish of Prestbury is principally pasture. The average rent is higher than in other counties being 30s. per acre. Leases seldom exceed seven years. The wages of labourers are in summer from 9s. to 15s. per week, in winter from 8s. to 10s. There is a considerable quantity of timber in the hedge rows, and a little beyond the limits of the parish, at Taxal, is one of the largest fir plantations in the county, covering 1,000 acres, planted at the cost of £5 per acre.

GEOLOGICAL NOTICE.

We are not aware that this district has been ever investigated by any eminent geologist, and are therefore not enabled to offer any accurate survey. A large portion of Cheshire is occupied by the new red stone, or red marl, which approaches Macclesfield on the west. The rocks of the coal strata extend on the east and the west of the town, and the millstone grit is first observed about four miles on the Buxton Road.

In the neighbourhood of Woodford is a considerable district of clay. The other parts of the hundred consist chiefly of sandy loam, with a great quantity of heath and peat moss.

There are quarries of sandstone at Styperson Park and Kerridge. The latter is called asiliceous grit with an argillaceous cement, and was formerly used for roofing houses.

Lead and copper ore, with some cobalt, connected with the veins in Alderley Edge, have been found at Mottram Andrew.

Collieries have been worked in the townships of Hurdsfield, Rainow, Bollington, Adlington, Shrigley, Lyme, and Worth. The seam of coal lies about 70 to 100 yards below the surface, and is usually found under a stratum of sandstone. The thickness of the bed very near Macclesfield is about two feet, at Worth and Poynton (where are the most considerable collieries) ten feet. A very large coal-pit at Shrigley, called Bakedale, is now disused.

KNIGHTS OF THE SHIRE.

1553 Edward Fitton, Gawsworth.
1601 Sir Peter Legh, Lyme.
1668 Richard Legh, Lyme.

1672 Sir Fulk Lucy, Henbury.
1806 Davies Davenport, Capesthorne.

SHERIFFS

OF THE COUNTY OF CHESTER.

1628 Thomas Legh, Adlington.
1630 Sir Edward Fitton, Gawsworth.
1643 Thomas Legh, Adlington.
1662 Thomas Legh, Adlington.
1681 Edward Downes, Shrigley.
1684 James Davenport, Woodford.
1688 Thomas Legh, Adlington.
1701 Laurence Wright, Mobberley.
1702 John Davenport, Woodford.
1704 John Baskervyle, Withington.

1724 Edward Downes, Shrigley.
1731 Edward Warren, Poynton.
1742 Peter Legh, Lyme.
1747 Charles Legh, Adlington.
1783 Davies Davenport, Capesthorne.
1788 John Glegg, Withington.
1798 Robert Hibbert, Birtles.
1802 Laurence Wright, Mottram.
1814 John Baskervyle Glegg, Gayton.

CLERGY

OF THE PARISH OF PRESTBURY.

Rev. John Rowlls Browne, Vicar, Prestbury.
Rev. J. W. Chaloner, Curate, Adlington Hall.
Rev. George Palmer, Bollington Cross.
Rev. G. Granville, Chelford.
Rev. R. H. Heptinstall, Fanshaw.
Rev. William Sutcliffe, Oaklands, North Rode.
Rev. W. C. Cruttenden, Parsonage House, Macclesfield.
Rev. J. Bradley, High Street, Sutton.
Rev. W. Pollock, Church Square, Macclesfield.
Rev. W. Brewster, ditto, ditto.
Rev. John Burnet, Foden Bank.
Rev. W. Hinson, Great King Street, Sutton.
Rev. W. A. Osborne, King Edward Street, Macclesfield.
Rev. J. B. Bennett, Chester Road.
Rev. J. Thornycroft, Thornycroft.
Rev. J. Mounsey, Fairfield, Buxton.
Rev. R. Litler, Poynton.
Rev. J. Darcey, Marton.
Rev. J. Sumner, Shrigley.
Rev. E. Luscombe, Saltersford.
Rev. W. Parke, Rainow.
Rev. J. Bostock, Cliffe Park, near Leek.

MAYORS OF MACCLESFIELD.

1768 Thomas Brock.
1769 T. Wright.
1770 William Clowes.
1771 Edward Shaw.
1772 E. Rowson.
1773 John Ryle.
1774 William Brooksbank.
1775 John Parker Moseley.
1776 Samuel Glover.
1777 Rowland Gould.
1778 Samuel Street.
1779 John Rowlls.
1780 John Rowlls (re-elected.)
1781 E. Lankford.
1782 J. Hawkins.
1783 William Harper.
1784 S. Wheldon.
1785 R. Deane.
1786 D. Hall.
1787 T. Vose.
1788 T. Whittaker.
1789 Thomas Hall.
1790 John Swanwick.
1791 Joseph Roe.
1792 Thomas Critchley.
1793 Robert Johnson.
1794 Jasper Hulley.
1795 Michael Daintry.
1796 John Smith Daintry.
1797 Francis Beswick.
1798 Thomas Allen.
1799 John Orme.
1800 Francis Newbold.
1801 S. Goodwin.
1802 N. Higginbotham,
1803 W. Stone.
1804 W. Ayton.

1805 { Davies-Davenport (refused.) / Thomas Brocklehurst.
1806 John Whitaker.
1807 H. Critchley.
1808 C. Wood.
1809 John Ryle.
1810 Edward Downes.
1811 Henry Wardle.
1812 John Rowlls Browne.
1813 George Pearson.
1814 Samuel Wood.
1815 Thomas Boden.
1816 Edward Smyth.
1817 Rowland Gould.
1818 Samuel Pearson.
1819 Ralph Deane.
1820 Ralph Deane (re-elected.)
1821 John W. Hazlehurst.
1822 Thomas Ward.
1823 Thomas Allen.
1824 George F. Baker.
1825 Thomas Brodrick.
1826 William Johnson.
1827 Samuel Pearson.
1828 Henry Wardle.
1829 W. B. Dickinson.
1830 Daniel Ward.
1831 W. Hopes.
1832 Thomas I. Watts.
1833 Thomas Grimsditch.
1834 John Fleet.
1835 Samuel Thorp.
1836 William Brocklehurst.
1837 Thomas Swanwick.
1838 W. Potts.
1839 Thomas Wardle.

BOROUGH POLICE-OFFICE.

GUILDHALL.—*Petty Sessions*—Monday, Wednesday, and Friday.

MAGISTRATES.

The Mayor.
The Ex-Mayor.
William Brocklehurst.
Thomas Brocklehurst.

Samuel Greg.
John Stansfield.
Thomas Swanwick, M.D.
Samuel Thorp.

COUNTY POLICE-OFFICE.

KING EDWARD STREET.—*Petty Sessions*—Tuesday.

MAGISTRATES.

Gibbs Crawfurd Antrobus.
John Brocklehurst.
Rev. W. Brownlow.
E. D. Davenport.
T. R. Daintry.
J. B. Glegg.
J. U. Gaskell.

Thomas Hibbert.
John Ryle.
John C. Ryle.
Clement Swettenham.
Lord Stanley of Alderley.
Hon. E. J. Stanley.
Thomas Swanwick, M.D.

There are Five Annual Fairs—On May 6, June 22, July 11, October 4, and November 11.

The Markets, (before 1815 held on Monday,) are now on Tuesday and Saturday.

The following *Coaches* start from Macclesfield daily :—

BETWEEN MANCHESTER AND MACCLESFIELD.

Fair Trader, 7 A. M. .... *Returns* 7 P. M.

The Hero, $\frac{1}{4}$ past 7 A. M. .... $\frac{1}{4}$ past 7 P. M.

True Briton, $\frac{1}{4}$ before 8 A. M. .... 8 P. M.

Brilliant, 9 A. M. .... 7 P. M.

BETWEEN MANCHESTER AND BIRMINGHAM.

Rover, 9 A. M. .... *Returns* 6 P. M.

BETWEEN LANE-END AND MANCHESTER.

Potter, 11 A. M. .... *Returns* 6 P. M.

BETWEEN UTTOXETER AND MANCHESTER.

The Express, 11 A. M. .... *Returns* $\frac{1}{2}$ past 1 P.M.

Post-Office, Mill Street—James Sargent, Postmaster. *Mail Cart* arrives at $\frac{1}{2}$ past 8 P. M.—Departs for Crewe Station at $\frac{1}{2}$ past 5 P. M.

J. Swinnerton, Printer, Macclesfield.

Lightning Source UK Ltd.
Milton Keynes UK
UKHW051244070223
416538UK00021B/421